DISCOVER
MEDITATION

DISCOVER
MEDITATION

A Practical Introduction to the Art
of Meditation

by

SIMON COURT

 Sterling Publishing Co., Inc. New York

Library of Congress Cataloging-in-Publication Data Available

1 3 5 7 9 10 8 6 4 2

Published 1994 by Sterling Publishing Company, Inc.
387 Park Avenue South, New York, N.Y. 10016
First published 1984 as *The Meditator's Manual*
This edition originally published 1992 in Great Britain by
The Aquarian Press, An Imprint of HarperCollins*Publishers*
© 1984 by Simon Court
Distributed in Canada by Sterling Publishing
% Canadian Manda Group, P.O. Box 920, Station U
Toronto, Ontario, Canada M8Z 5P9
Manufactured in the United States of America
All rights reserved

Sterling ISBN 0-8069-0640-5

Contents

Acknowledgements

The illustrations were provided by Maggie Maylin who also typed the manuscript.

The Theosophical Society provided the opportunity to conduct the course on which this book is based. The participants in those courses upheld my belief that this system works.

To all of these, I thank you.

Introduction

Much has been written about meditation and meditation practices and this literary plethora has effectively produced a bewildering array of methods and systems, each making its own claims and promises. Such a great variety of offerings has tended either to dazzle the beginner into inactivity through indecision or to fulfil a dilettante need for a constant supply of distractions enabling the practitioner to dally at the beginnings of meditation practice and avoid the threat of real self-unfolding.

This book therefore does not offer a system of meditation but rather seeks to provide a set of exercises which represent the building blocks out of which the various systems are constructed. No claims are made for the exercises, for it is only the practitioners themselves who can experience their effects.

This book then is a journey of self-discovery, combining practical examples in the form of exercises with suggestions about the nature of ourselves in relation to the universe that provide a basis for ordering and understanding the experiences obtained with regular meditation practice.

When you have completed the various exercises you will know more about meditation than could have been told to you in a book of this size. The Chinese used to say: 'One showing is worth a thousand tellings.' This book seeks to *show* you meditation by a planned series of demonstrations upon what must be potentially one of the most wonderful systems in all creation – yourself.

1
Meditation

What is meditation?

There are as many answers to this question as there are people who meditate. No matter what may be said about meditation, the only person who can really answer the question is you yourself: only through your own experiences can you really know anything at all. **This book therefore presents a** series of exercises which will give you an experience of meditation as it relates to you. These exercises do not represent a particular 'brand' of meditation, nor are they the teachings of any particular school.

Each of the various styles of meditation which we might find 'on the market' these days is made up of a number of different types of practice. When we reduce these practices down to their basic elements we find that there are about eight fundamental techniques that go to make up a balanced meditation practice. The methods offered by the various teachers and schools are usually built out of a combination of these basic facets.

This book is designed as a course that you can follow at your own rate. Each chapter introduces an exercise based upon one of the fundamental techniques and provides information that complements the exercise and helps you to understand it. In this way you are able to concentrate upon one aspect at a time, experiencing its effects over a period of time chosen to suit yourself. At the end of that time you will be able to assess how well the particular technique suits your own needs and circumstances.

When you complete this course of practices you will find that some of the exercises suit you whereas others do not seem to work for you at all. On the basis of this you will be able to devise a meditation practice which is tailor-made for you as an individual. It may be that what you put together turns out to be very similar to the practices offered by a particular school or teacher. If you come to hear about such a group then you may have found the teachings that can help you further along the way.

Through regular and diligent practice of your chosen meditation style, you will awaken to activity those inner parts of yourself that had previously lain dormant. In so doing, you will bring yourself to the attention of the forces which exist behind this world and which constantly inspire all true teachers of meditation. Whether you personally consider these forces to be people who have gone before us, archetypal drives towards evolution within ourselves or cosmic energies which inspire all mystics and teachers, is quite immaterial. You will be drawn into contact with people who use similar methods of meditation to the one you have constructed, by a form of magnetization. This is in fact the process that brings people of like paths closer together.

Now a word about the way in which this book is structured.

Each chapter contains:

— an exercise for you to do;
— an outline of some appropriate aspect of life;
— feedback from other people's experiences with the exercise, drawn from workshop sessions conducted by the author.

The exercise is given for you to practise before proceeding further. Each exercise is given in a particular order and should be undertaken in sequence, as each experience builds upon those encountered previously. You may, of course, choose to read the book through without doing the exercises. However, in doing this you will lose much of the benefit of this book. This is a *practical* manual of meditation technique and as you progress through each stage you will gain in knowledge, bringing you to a deeper understanding of the later parts of the book soundly based upon what you have already achieved. Indeed, the later chapters may well prove unintelligible without this.

Here is the difference between 'knowing' and merely 'knowing about'. Many who are content to remain academic spectators will dismiss the reality known by participators simply because they themselves do not have the experiential background to see that reality. Such people live their lives second-hand at best.

Each chapter then has an exercise for you to undertake until you feel that you are happy to proceed. As a general rule you should aim to complete at least ten sessions within a period of two weeks. You should set aside a period of 10–15 minutes each day for your practice. This in itself can be quite a challenge. Obviously, circumstances arise which make the missing of a session unavoidable, but our own inner resistance to new experiences can sometimes engineer these. If possible, the time you set aside should be in the same section of your living cycle on each occasion.

The most generally effective times have been found to be just after rising, before eating a meal and just before going to bed. Make sure that you will not be disturbed, make yourself comfortable, touch your tongue lightly to your palate, settle into yourself, relax and close your eyes and you are ready to begin your practice proper. When you have finished the session, write down as soon as possible your experiences and realizations. This can be done in the table provided at the end of each chapter, or you may prefer to build your own personal record and copy the tables into a notebook kept specially for the purpose, allowing sufficient space for you to enter your experiences.

Here we must mention a very important point. Most of us live in a hectic world in our everyday life. This demands the exercise of numerous skills, concentration and a way of thinking that is different, in the early stages, to the state of mind induced by regular meditation practice. Even if your lifestyle is fairly relaxed this difference in mental processes still exists, but to a lesser degree. The practice of meditation can introduce two related yet distinct dangers in this respect. On the one hand, the meditative state of mind may lead us away from what we are doing in the world and the commitments we have already undertaken. On the other hand, however, the vigour and mundane practicality of our workaday life may overpower the tender shoot of meditative consciousness. Both of these problems are known technically as 'leakage' between planes of conscious existence or so-called states of consciousness. We therefore provide a psychological device to prevent this from occurring.

Before beginning each session of meditation make a gesture with the hands as though parting or opening a pair of curtains. Then at the end of each session you will symbolically close the curtains again. This device will ensure that the two types of consciousness remain distinct. The meditative consciousness, as it becomes stronger and more stable within you, will begin to overshadow and influence your normal life, but without contamination. This is a very important point and on no account should it be neglected. It is the failure to use any such device that has brought many of the negative views held by non-meditators, for these people have not reacted favourably to the unbalanced changes that have occurred in their meditating associates as a result of their practices. Of course, these attitudes sometimes are attributable to the limited viewpoint held by people who have not practised techniques of self-development, but not always.

When you complete your period of practice and again take up this book, you will find a 'feedback' section at the beginning of the next chapter in sequence. This provides you with a list of the experiences that other people have encountered in workshop sessions with that particular technique which you have just used. From this list you will be able to see which of your own experiences might be shared or universal and which might be purely your own unique relationship with the exercise.

This list of experiences, by the way, is not a set of 'right answers', nor is it intended to show development towards or away from some hypothetical desired result. To make any such claim would be to tailor your own experiences to some devised model and thereby impose that model upon you. Such an approach is against the whole philosophy behind the teaching of meditation. It is true that a personal meditation teacher would give students an indication about the directions in which their studies and practices were leading them, this being after the fashion of guidance in the unique self-unfolding of each individual. With this book, however, the position is somewhat different, for you are acting, with assistance, as your own teacher. Since it is the teacher that is responsible for the development of the student, then in following this course you are responsible for the learning that you derive from your own experiences. You are, at centre, an evolving, unfolding and self-regulating being. Having had an experience you cannot then *un*-have it, although you may repress or ignore it. Experiences become part of your make-up, part of what you are, and this is automatically taken into account by your natural self-regulating processes – physical and psychic. The list of experiences of other meditators is in general provided merely to show that some of your experiences may have been shared by others, while some may be purely personal. Personal experiences are not in any way invalid. They are just personal experiences in exactly the same way as the list provided represents the purely personal experiences of those who used these exercises during a series of courses run as workshop sessions. Every experience is valid as something from which we may learn. What we learn from each one is up to us.

Each style of meditation practice given has some more or less firm correspondence with some faculty of our psyche or inner make-up. To the degree that we live in harmony with the world around us, to that extent do we also recognize the correspondence between our inner nature and the things of the outside world. Each chapter presents a series of ideas about these inner and outer powers and faculties that relate in some way to the exercise being performed. These ideas are not put forward as a dogmatic statement of how things are. They are merely this author's own views offered for your consideration. You may accept or reject them as you wish, for this is your own choice. The way of the true seeker after wisdom is the holding of opinions and theories lightly. In this way, new ideas can be taken up on a 'trial basis' and kept as long as they remain useful as explanations or categories for making sense out of experience. However, when found wanting they should be modified, expanded or rejected in favour of some more effective view. This is far preferable a practice to that of uncritically embracing or rejecting wholeheartedly everything that comes to our attention. It is in the spirit of their possible usefulness that the ideas in each chapter are offered and they should be considered in this light.

The Exercise

The first exercise must be a preliminary look at your thoughts and expectations about meditation before you start your course proper. This exercise, though simple, is basic and essential to the whole method and should not be neglected or avoided. It has two parts, the first of which is to be performed for at least six sessions, the remaining sessions being devoted to the second practice which, as you will see, is based upon the results obtained.

Part One
Make sure that you will not be disturbed; sit or lie in a comfortable position and begin to relax your body by starting at the top of the head and working downwards. Move your attention down through the face and neck, shoulders and arms, chest, back and abdomen. Then continue on down the thighs, knees, calves, ankles, feet and toes. Check all of the muscles you can feel, one after the other, deliberately relaxing them before passing on. There should be no sense of strain in the process. You should firmly hold the conviction that the muscles *will* relax as your attention leaves them. Spend a little time and care making sure you are as relaxed physically as possible.

Now, in your relaxed state, retain your mental concentration and ponder upon your reasons for wanting to practise meditation. There are probably many reasons that will present themselves; merely note mentally what they are and continue probing to ensure that you allow as many of them as possible to come into the light of consciousness. After each session write down whatever has come to you as a reason – or reasons – for wanting to learn or take up meditation. Even if you come up with several reasons during the first session, try to persevere right through to the end of the six sessions to give an opportunity for deeper messages about yourself to arise.

Part Two
Record a summary of your reasons in Table 1 at the end of this chapter. Then,

for the remaining sessions, take each of your reasons in turn and work out for each one what would have to happen to show that you had definitely succeeded in that aim. In a similar way, determine what would definitely indicate failure. You must be as precise and practical as possible in this: it is not sufficient just to *feel* that you have or have not succeeded. Try to express these tests in terms of specific changes that will occur in you and in your life situation. Actual measurable or identifiable events are preferable to subjective evaluations. If your goal is 'to be more relaxed', how exactly would this show in your day-to-day behaviour and attitudes?

Now record your test descriptions alongside each of your aspirations. Take time and care over this exercise as we shall return to this table at the end of the course.

Table 1
Reasons for wanting to practise meditation

Date:	This will show I have attained it	This will show I have failed to attain it
My reasons for doing a course of meditation are:		
What I want out of meditation is:		

Summary

— You can come to know what meditation is at first hand through your own experiencing.
— Practise at the same time each day.
— Aim to complete at least ten sessions of 10–15 minutes each within a two-week period.
— Begin each session with the opening gesture and finish each session with the closing gesture.
— Practise the exercises and record your results *before* proceeding further.

2
The Real World

Feedback

Over the last few days you have looked within yourself and examined your reasons for wanting to take a course in meditation. Now look back at what you have written and compare your expectations with those given by others who have been asked this question in meditation sessions.

— To gain relaxation.
— Finding a method which motivates me.
— Gaining an incentive to continue meditating.
— I want to find myself, to gain self-knowledge and self-realization.
— I want to broaden the meditation technique I already have.
— To gain knowledge of different techniques and philosophies.
— To find out more about meditation.
— To get the benefits of meditation.
— To help me cope with stress.
— To help me see things as they really are.
— I want to develop a more harmonious relationship with the universe.
— Meditation will help me withdraw into myself.
— To gain stability.
— I feel it will give me guidance from within.
— To improve my concentration.
— I want to use my meditation for refreshment when I am tired.
— I can use my meditation to live and cope happily when I am alone.

As you can see from this list, meditation is generally reckoned by many people to be something of a universal panacea. Perhaps you would like to consider how the people who expressed some of those aspirations might have devised tests of success and failure. By now you will have discovered for yourself something of the difficulty involved in anchoring lofty aspirations firmly to the ground!

The Real World

When you get right down to it, there are not many people who would doubt the reality of the world that surrounds us and in which we normally live and move. Pundits who popularize their own versions of the Eastern theories of nature remind us that all is in fact *maya*, or illusion. Be that as it may, there are very few of them or us who can actually *behave* as though this were so; for when you stub your toe, you encounter an object quite solid and real. The pain too is real.

Rather than consider this real world itself, let us talk about our experiences of it. Every one of our perceptions about the world is conveyed to us by our senses. These are the physical senses of smell, taste, sight, hearing, touch and body position. Every apparent object and event in the world is known to us only through these organs of perception and the nervous system. It is important also to remember that your own physical body is similarly an object in the world that may be seen, touched, and so on. We view the world as though there is something 'out there' like houses and trees, cars and mountains, seas and sewers. By some miraculous means our sense organs then convey information about these things to our waiting mind. We have established a consensus with other human beings over what is to be classed as 'real' and what is not to be so classed. This conspiracy of agreement lends credence to the idea that there really is something 'out there'.

Or is there? Is this the only way of looking at it? Suppose just for the moment that there is some universal central source that transmits information about all things and all times. Suppose too that the mind, or the consciousness, is somehow 'tuned in' to this source to a greater or lesser extent. On the basis of the information received, we 'construct' our version of reality. It would not then be surprising that there would be consensus with our fellow humans, more or less, for we all have the same basic make-up and faculties, and we all have similar access, under this view, to that single source. We could then consider matter to be a blank screen upon which we project our own images made up from the information we have received from this hypothetical One Source. Where these various images overlap we have agreement, and this is usually the case with 'actual objects'. But the correspondence is not perfect, for there are those who can see, and agree with others upon, energy fields, auras, nature spirits, and so on. There are those who can hear other people's thoughts, locate underground water or detect illnesses in others. There is surprising agreement amongst the mystics of different times, cultures and religions as to the nature of existence and the experience of cosmic consciousness. Yet their views are quite different to those of us who have a more restricted vision.

Furthermore, we appear to be either spectators or participators in the world. We seem to choose to be either audience or actor. When we act on the world, other people generally perceive our actions and we view each other as responsible agents bringing about changes. We therefore have access to this information that comes from the central source and from which reality is constructed in a manner that allows us to manipulate it. We make a distinction between those things under our control – such as moving, talking, kicking a ball, and so on, and those apparently beyond our control – such as the wind which blows the newspaper away. Our legal, moral and ethical values are based upon these distinctions.

However, given this alternative view of reality we can see that we are in fact responsible for *all* of reality. The fact that we can apparently only influence a part of it is immaterial, for the faults we see around us might well be errors in the way we have interpreted and used the information of that central source. This view then makes us all responsible for the world around us, regardless of the amount of control we feel we have.

It is no good saying that others agree with us about the world, for we construct reality in a similar way to those around us. Things which upset or offend us often upset or offend the majority of the local or national population. It is on the basis of our values that we work the magic of constructing shared reality. Where values differ so do the respective realities.

Why is this important? What has this to do with meditation? Quite simply put, meditation will change your values. Be warned that it may change the way that you see things. This does not mean that you will suddenly start seeing green sky and pink grass. But it does mean that things which previously offended you might no longer do so. And things which seemed quite normal and natural to you once upon a time might begin to offend you. This could result in changes to your circle of friends and associates, for it is the closely shared reality based upon a similar set of values that draws us together – even if one of those values is the need to differ, divide and argue. The changes that may become necessary during meditation are the result of the mechanism referred to above by which those who practise similar methods of meditation come closer together.

Now this alternative view of reality makes each of us responsible for the world as we see it. Reality for us is a mirror that reflects back to us what we are like. Without this knowledge it is not possible for us to change ourselves – and change ourselves we must, for, in the words of the Dutch proverb, 'To change the world you must start with yourself.' If we reject the idea that the world is a mirror of one's own self and treat it as though it had an independent existence in the form in which we perceived it, then we would not have to change. We could put all the blame for our own faults on to other people and outside circumstances. If, however, we can view the world and say, 'This is a mirror of me. This is what I am like myself,' then we have the possibility of change. We have begun to take responsibility for ourselves and we can begin to change the world by changing ourselves.

There is a story that tells of a divine child who found a mirror amongst his toys. This child became so fascinated by the wealth of images he found therein of his own reflection that he ignored all of his other toys. We are like that child. Enraptured by the world, we treat it as though it had independent existence. It is, of course, real – as we *experience* it, in all its pleasure and pain. These experiences, however, are of our own making and derive from the way that we react to the reality that we have constructed. By changing the way that we do this, we change our perceptions and our experiences. We must first, though, become more aware of that constructed reality. In this way, we become able to observe it more accurately and thus to begin to see the connections between what is 'inside' and what is 'outside' and how the one influences the other. Until we become aware of what is happening around us we cannot be aware of what is inside us. The one comes from the other.

The Exercise

This meditation exercise will help you to increase your awareness. It is called breath counting. Don't be fooled by the name: it is not quite so simple as it first appears. Its effects can be most profound. You may already have practised it in exactly the way it is described here.

For your exercise you should get into a comfortable position, begin with your opening sign or gesture, relax as you have already learned and turn your attention to your breathing. Do not try to influence it in any way. Feel how the air moves into your mouth and nose, moves down your throat, expands into your lungs. Notice all the details of how your chest and belly move as the air flows into and out of your lungs. Remember, do *not* try to change the breathing pattern. Do not try to keep it the same either: if the pattern starts to change, merely observe and note the change. What you are doing is observing without meddling: you are allowing the breath to flow as it will, naturally. Whilst you merely watch, continue in this way, feeling the air; feeling the body movements; watching as a passive observer. This is the first part of the exercise and when you can do this you are ready to begin the meditation proper. This you do by counting the breaths that you observe. Count once for each in-breath and once for each out-breath. Each time your attention wanders, bring it back gently to the counting process again. Do not be concerned about any thoughts that may come into your mind. It is sufficient to realize that the mind is wandering without pursuing what arises. If you lose count of your breaths, then begin from one again. It is a very simple exercise.

Try this exercise for a few moments, right now, and note the experiences that you have. Put the book down now and try it.

A common experience that people have with this exercise is that the counting becomes fixed, regular and mechanical. The breathing then falls in line with it. Try to avoid this if you can. The breathing should be natural and that means not interfered with or brought under control in any way. In fact, the counting will not be regular. Natural breathing will change its pace as you watch. The idea is to watch in a somewhat disinterested fashion.

Over the period of the practice try to achieve at first a goal of twenty breaths counted, then fifty, then one hundred. Record the count reached in Table 2. After this add one hundred each time as your new target. Surprisingly enough, most people find that to manage fifty is a considerable achievement. Remember to record the details of each practice session and to do all the sessions before the next chapter.

Table 2
Breath Counting

Session	Date	Time	Place	Count reached
1				
2				
3				
4				
5				
6				
7				
8				
9				
10				
11				
12				
13				
14				

Other experiences

Summary

— We can consider the outside world as constructed by our own selves.
— There is a reality out of which we make a representation which contains distortions.
— This representation is projected upon pure matter which thereby reflects back to us what we are really like.
— We can change the world by changing ourselves.
— To do this properly we must first become more aware of the world as we see it.
— Practise the exercise and record your results *before* proceeding to the next chapter.

3
The Inner World

Feedback

We are now ready to review the experiences from the last series of meditations. Although what happens to someone during the meditation is a personal and individual thing, you will often find that others have had a similar experience to yourself. Some of our experiences occur at a personal level and some at what might be called a 'transpersonal' level. Here for comparison are some of the experiences that people have had with the breath counting meditation in actual workshop conditions.

— All of a sudden I went blank and images came.
— Everything went blank and then nothing.
— Wandering off, trains of thoughts, a barrage of thoughts.
— It was irritating to count. Watching was far better.
— One session was very long, much longer than it seemed, with a dream or something in the middle.
— A beautiful feeling welled up inside of me. I had a feeling of expansiveness.
— Thoughts came rushing through, very very rapidly.
— I felt a steady stream of thoughts.
— I experienced the thoughts and the counting at the same time. I did not know this was possible.
— I saw flashes of colour and complementary effects, tunnels and spirallings and spinnings.
— It was peaceful and calm. I felt very refreshed.
— I was distracted by a lot of outside noises.
— I kept wanting to do something else.

Perhaps you shared some of these experiences and perhaps not. In either case you might ask yourself what your own experiences might mean in terms of your being an agent in constructing reality. How do they relate, if at all, to your responsibility to become more aware of that reality?

The breathing process is one that we can either control deliberately or allow to happen in its own course. In a sense, this process is half-way between the areas that we can control and those that we cannot. When we do not think of our breathing, it follows its own pattern correctly and without pause. We can, however, take charge of the process and breathe according to a prescribed rate.

Breathing brings the outside world inside of us. We bring outside air into our lungs where it contacts the inner surface of our own self before being exhaled and going out into the world again. So breathing represents a boundary between two different levels of being. Remember that thought seems to exert control over some aspects of the world and not others, yet we are responsible for everything that occurs in our perceptions.

Breathing is what might then be called a boundary process illustrating to us that there are events which may either follow a natural pattern or be influenced by our own efforts. Such processes straddle the boundary between the realms of awareness and non-awareness. If we wish to extend our degree of control into new areas then we shall have to extend our awareness into the areas of existence of which we do not as yet have direct knowledge.

The Inner World

When we close our eyes and withdraw our senses from the world around us we enter another realm entirely. It has strange laws that govern its events for here all is fluid rather than solid, and time has quite a different meaning. It is the world in which we dream. It is here that we ponder our future, muse upon the past, daydream and play out our most secret fantasies. In this realm, all stories, myths and legends are true and will live again as we recall them.

In the myths of most cultures there are stories of how things were before the world of our normal experience came into being. From the great creation themes of the Navajo Indian emergence story to the book of Genesis, these all tell how the transition occurred from one mode of existence to another, from the heaven worlds to the earth. This prior existence the Australian Aborigines called 'the dreamtime' and this is an excellent term for this realm for many reasons.

We so-called civilized people have learned a certain way of viewing things that is not the only way. One of our masterful creations is history – the idea of a linear progression in the unfolding of knowledge and expansion and civilization. We refer to certain prior times as 'pre-historic' or 'primitive', meaning earlier along this progression with all that that implies. We recognize that some cultures, even today, do not have a 'history' as we know it. Of course, we are able to supply it for such cultures from outside, but within those groups time was conceived cyclically in seasonal progressions which were celebrated according to crop patterns or game movements. When the people of a tribe gathered together to celebrate the rebirth of the light at the winter solstice, they were joined in a timeless moment with all the other times that this ceremony occurred and with all times that it was yet to be celebrated. Past and future coalesced into an eternal instant, pregnant with cosmic significance.

We have come to think of creation myths as trying to express some long-distant event at the very beginning of history, and this may well be valid. But in addition to this we must realize that the dreamtime, the heaven world, the realm of the ancestors, still exists right now, side by side with the world of normal experience. The shaman visits this world to talk with ancestors as easily today as his forerunners themselves did in times past.

When we get away from our limited conception of linear time we see that the creation myths refer to an ongoing process. The world about us is still being created and nourished from moment to moment by this underlying heaven world. In this realm we find not only the ancestors of people but also the ancestors of events in the world. That is, we find here the causes behind this everyday world of phenomena. People we have disparagingly referred to as 'primitive' were aware that all causation proceeded from this realm. Our sophisticated science on the other hand has sought to explain phenomena purely in terms of other phenomena. It is only recently that our scientists have begun to see the causation realm beyond the limits to which they have pushed their investigations. Between the primitives and the moderns, one wonders who is closer to the truth.

There is then a realm of causes and a set of creation stories which tell us the actual process by which the one realm translates into the other, had we wit enough to understand them. It is this realm that we enter when we withdraw from the outside world and put our creative imagination to work. It is this faculty which will bring the dreamtime alive to us and make it as real as the outside world.

There are many schools of 'positive thought' that have shown how to obtain the objects of our desires by using this faculty of the creative imagination. These methods work and they work by using the natural laws of the universe. For whatever you create vividly in the dreamtime will come about in the world in exactly the same way as is continually occurring outside our normal awareness. This dreamtime world is not after all a separate state of mind. It is a concurrent mode of thought and existence. The difference lies only in where we direct our attention.

We can, then, enter this realm in the same way that the shaman and witch-doctor have done for countless centuries. We have only to direct our attention inward as fixedly as possible. It is not necessary to go into a trance in order to do this, for the dreamtime world is very easily accessible to us. It is from this realm that our greatest artists have taken their inspiration. In continual application of the archetypal images and themes found there, they have modified those images into the current day's context, causing an influence back upon the dreamtime which expands and enlivens those archetypes.

It is in the dreamtime world that the information sent out by that deep central source finds form with which to clothe itself. The forms and images we place there ourselves will be used by that source to the extent that they 'fit' – and they fit the more closely as they align with archetypal themes. Manipulation of this realm brings changes in the world around us.

Those who practise meditation as a method of spiritual development are more concerned with working upon themselves than seeking directly to influence the outside realm. For it is in oneself that the roots of problems and suffering lie. There are methods of meditation that are designed to make changes in the dreamtime world in order to effect changes in the practitioners themselves. Of course, these methods may also be used for winning lotteries or gaining promotions in one's job and so on. There is nothing wrong in this at all – provided that it is not done *instead* of work on the self. You should always use your talents to aid you in your quest, and comfortable surroundings – together with a lifestyle not constrained by unnecessary economic limitations – go a long way to providing a suitable setting for self-development practices. The ethical key to the whole matter is that such measures should not be undertaken at the expense, or to the harm, of any living being. This includes yourself.

The Exercise

In the exercise for the next practice period you will be using the creative imagination to work upon your own nature, but indirectly. There are many methods which use this technique. Three are given here and you may choose any one of them. Under no circumstances, however, should you mix up these systems. By all means try one for ten sessions followed by another for a further ten sessions and so forth if you wish to sample them all for comparison purposes. You should not, however, 'chop and change'.

The first exercise is part of the Western mystery tradition and has its foundation in the Qabalah. The second is from Indian sources and has its basis in the doctrines of the Yoga Chakra systems. The third is derived from the Taoist alchemical texts of China and is based upon the circulation of vital force in what we today would call the acupuncture meridians of the body. These systems appear at first sight to use different and contradictory methods. There is, however, no conflict, for there are in the human form a great number of energy centres and connecting channels which run between them. Some methods concentrate on one set of these, some on another and others on groupings that are different again. Several systems have been found to work, and this is the important point. It is the extent to which they work that proves their effectiveness and it is from this that they derive their value for a given person in a given time and place.

Western Method

Let us begin with the exercise taken from the Western mystery tradition. It is called the 'middle pillar' exercise and symbolically draws energy from the source of all, through various stages of being and into manifestation. It may be performed whilst standing, sitting in a chair, or sitting cross-legged – but *not* in the lotus position, or padmasana, of hatha yoga.

Relax the body, breathing easily and deeply. Turn your attention inward, ready to use your picture-making imagination. As you breathe in, imagine a sphere of vibrant white light to expand and form so that its centre is just above the head. Breathe in and out a few times, feeling the energy build as the breath is taken in and seeing the image stabilize as the breath is let out. When you feel ready, imagine as you are breathing out that a shaft of brilliant white light descends from the head sphere to the location of the throat. On the next in-breath, see a sphere of brilliant pulsing white light expand here too. Pause here, breathing in and out, building the energy and the images. When you are ready, continue on downwards on an out-breath once more, progressing in this way to solar plexus, genitals and ground beneath the feet. The correct locations are shown in Figures 1–3.

Pause for a moment here with all five spheres shining brilliantly on that central shaft. Then, when you feel that the power and energy is fully gathered in the ground centre, let it begin to ascend on the next in-breath up the shaft right to the head centre again. On the next out-breath, see this light energy spray out high above your head like a fountain. On the next in-breath, the light

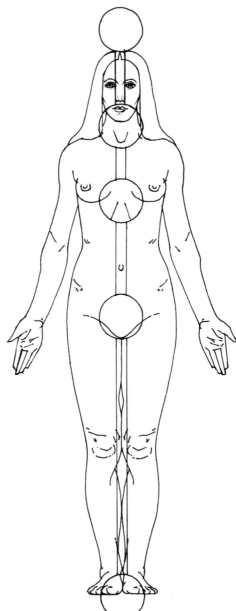

Figure 1
Middle pillar exercise: Standing

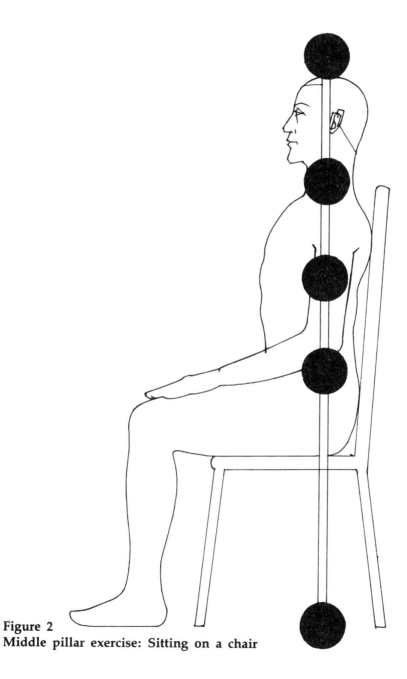

Figure 2
Middle pillar exercise: Sitting on a chair

Figure 3
Middle pillar exercise: Sitting cross-legged

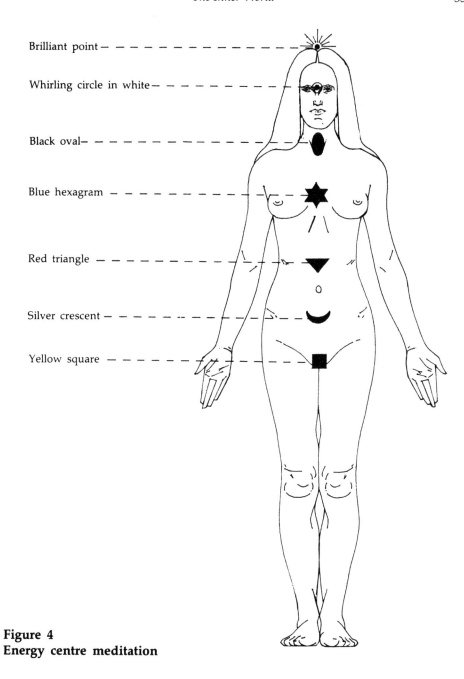

Brilliant point — — — — — — — — —

Whirling circle in white — — — — — — —

Black oval — — — — — — — — — —

Blue hexagram — — — — — — —

Red triangle — — — — — — — —

Silver crescent — — — — — — — —

Yellow square — — — — — — —

Figure 4
Energy centre meditation

begins to fall back all around you at the distance of your outstretched hands. On the next out-breath, this liquid light accumulates and gathers once more at the ground centre. Continue this fountain effect for at least six circuits to end finally on an in-breath which draws all back up into the head centre again.

Indian Method

The second technique is taken from certain yogic practices having their origin in India. The general term for these methods is 'Chakra Dharana' or energy centre meditation. This exercise may be performed standing, seated in a chair or whilst sitting cross-legged.

Relax the body, breathing easily and deeply. Turn your attention inward ready to use the pictorial imagination. As you breathe in, build in the mind's eye the picture of a yellow square. Breathe in and out a few times to intensify and stabilize the image. Then, on an out-breath, see the yellow square pass down the spinal column to take up its place at the base of the spine. Breathing in, build the picture of a silver crescent. Pause for a few breaths to stabilize the image before sending it too down the spinal column to a point about 40 mm below the navel. Next, a red triangle is formed in the same manner and sent to its location level within the solar plexus. A blue six-pointed star, like two interlaced triangles, is placed at the level of the heart, followed by a black oval at the throat position. A small white whirling circle is then formed and left in place in the space behind and between the eyes. Finally, a brilliant tiny point of light appears at the top of the head.

This completes the exercise which can be repeated a number of times to make up the practice period. Figure 4 illustrates the shapes and their apparent locations upon the body.

Chinese Method

The last technique for you to consider is taken from the methods of Taoist alchemy, which has its origin in Chinese systems of health and self-development. The general term for this practice is 'microcosmic circulations' and it is the preliminary step of a complete and very ancient method of gaining enlightenment. However, this exercise taken alone does indeed produce its own special benefits. It may be performed seated in a chair, whilst sitting cross-legged, or kneeling down seated upon the backs of the ankles.

Relax the body, breathing easily and deeply. Turn your attention inward ready to use your creative visualizing faculties. As you breathe in, imagine a sphere of light to appear inside your head. Breathe in and out a few times to stabilize the image. When you are ready breathe out, transferring your attention downwards to a point halfway between the genitals and the anus. This point is the location of the sphincter muscle and it is called 'the gate of birth and death'. Here a small sphere of light forms. As you breathe in, this sphere of light ascends vertically upwards through the centre of the body to the level of the heart. Breathe out and allow the light-energy to descend to the gate once more. Continue this pumping action up and down the central channel until you feel proficient in its practice. Throughout this practice, the sphere of light within the head should be visualized as continuing to exist in its place.

Having brought the force back to the gate of birth and death on an out-breath, you are now ready to proceed with the second stage of the exercise.

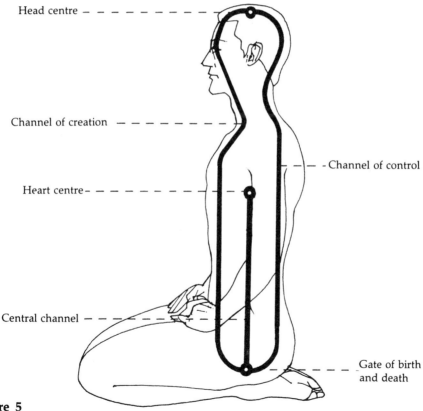

Figure 5
Microcosmic circulations

Breathing in, see the light ascend up the spine until it reaches the original sphere within the head, joining with it. On the out-breath, bring the light down the front of the body back to the gate again. Continue in this way taking the energy up the spine through the channel of control on each in-breath and bringing it down the front of the body through the channel of creation on each out-breath for the remainder of the session. These paths are illustrated in Figure 5. To complete the exercise, take one last in-breath, raising the light up the central channel to the heart, lowering it again to the gate on the out-breath. Reaffirm that the sphere of light inside your head is still present, and the exercise is over.

General Notes

It may be helpful for some people to build these exercises up gradually over a number of sessions rather than tackling them in their entirety at the first try. Each one divides easily into a number of steps that can be worked out to suit your own capacity to visualize and to remember the instructions. You could, of course, record the instructions onto a cassette tape with suitable pauses. This is quite permissible for your own private use and may prove an effective means of mastering the technique.

It is essential to remember that you are working upon the dreamtime world rather than the so-called physical world. The descriptions of the body and spine are to indicate corresponding locations. On no account should you imagine these images to be within the actual physical body as this will weaken their effectiveness and lead to confusion.

Record your results after each session in Table 3 so that you have a proper record of your progress. Set down a summary of your experiences at the end of the practice period before proceeding further. Take note of all effects – physical and emotional, inner and outer.

Table 3
The Inner World

Method used	Immediate effects	After-effects

Summary

— The dreamtime world exists here and now, concurrently with the world of normal experience.

— Creation myths explain how the world of sense is continually being created and sustained by the dreamtime realm.

— We enter this other realm through the creative imagination. Changes made there bring about changes in the world.

— We use proven symbolic visualization techniques to work upon and modify our own selves and thereby affect indirectly the world around us.

— Practise the exercise and record your results *before* proceeding to the next chapter.

4
The World of Thoughts

Feedback

Here are some of the things that people said about this exercise when it was conducted in various workshop sessions.

— I had energy in my hands and arms.
— It gave me a sense of life.
— I felt a great pulsing in me.
— I felt energy moving and cleansing me.
— I felt very poised and balanced.
— I found some shapes harder to visualize than others.
— I couldn't control the shapes very well and the whole thing wasn't very stable.
— I felt a flying sensation and felt very light.
— I suddenly saw a dim white light all around me.
— I could not see the shapes in three dimensions.
— I felt aroused sexually.
— I could feel the play of energies between each centre.
— I got a great rush of energy and a tingling in my fingers.
— I felt a vibration in my eardrums like a low sound.
— At one point I was overcome with a feeling of panic.
— I broke out in a sweat.

The World of Thoughts

So far we have considered existence in terms of a duality between a world seen as real and outside of ourselves and an inner dream world of fantasy found within. We have seen how the inner world contains the causes which eventually produce their effects in the world of physical sensation. Remember that these two realms coexist, the difference being in where our attention is directed. It is a useful device, however, to treat them separately for a while in order that we may understand them more fully.

So having divided, for the moment, what is essentially one thing, we can consider the interplay that exists between these realms and their communication one with the other.

We use many faculties to represent that which we find in the inner world. Painting, poetry, music and dance are very popular and universal means of representation. In order for us to associate a particular item with the inner reality it is intended to represent, we must see something enduring and recognizable in that item. It is through the form or structure of such representations that we achieve this. In the case of a dance, it would have certain steps to be performed in a certain sequence, albeit allowing individual variations within prescribed limits. This dance would then represent our experience. A different dance would represent a different experience.

Ritual dance, ritual painting and ritual artifacts have always been sacred in their make-up or structure. They must always be performed or executed in the same way each time without change or modification. This applies equally to the sand paintings of the Navajo as to the ikons of the Orthodox Church. Storytelling too is such an art and it is the form or structure of the stories that enables us to find similarities between the legends of the Australian Aborigines, the Greeks, the Celts and many others, regardless of the variations in local content.

Language itself is just one of those methods of representation. However, at a certain stage of 'civilized' history the word, both spoken and written, began to gain supremacy as the medium for representing experience. This process was rapidly accelerated by the invention of the printing press. In time, the form of words and their combinations became more regular in structure. Variations diminished and dropped away completely.

In the time of Chaucer there were many ways of spelling the same words. Now this no longer occurs; or, rather, it is seen as a departure from correct form when it does occur. Grammar, which began as a description of the structure existing in language, now dictates forms and word order. What began as description has now become prescription – a set of rules – for the use of language. This is using a cart to pull a horse. For only the illiterate now keep language as a living process whereas the researchers who perceive its deficiencies must fight for change against the laws of grammar – 'proper usage' – that have stifled linguistic growth. Spelling and semantic reforms meet considerable opposition, and terms like the non-sexist singular 'they', still used in parts of England, cannot get back into a grammar that once chose to ignore them as aberrations. Here we have formalism which has gone too far, for it has become a tyrant, changing its recording role to a regulatory one. This is a danger with all forms, from personal language to national government.

When we wish to communicate our experiences of either the inner or outer world to each other, or even to ourselves for our own enlightenment, we must use some means of representing those experiences. We must attach to each experience a pattern of movements or sounds or shapes or colours. We can call this pattern the 'name' of the experience, for it stands for the experience in the same way that the name of someone stands for that person but yet 'is not' them. The advantage of doing this is that we may deal with the experience symbolically at a time other than that at which the awareness occurred which gave rise to that experience. This then is the development of thought, which is a different creature again to both the inner and outer worlds. It should be apparent, though it is often forgotten, that thought deals with representations of things rather than the things themselves. Thought enables us to deal symbolically with experiences that have already happened, making memory and history possible. Thought allows us to construct symbolically experiences that we have not had. This introduces the ability to create falsehoods. It also enables us to create 'supposings' and thereby gives birth to the scientific method that has given us today's technology, for good or ill.

Thought has no in-built value system but merely deals with symbolic representations according to its own laws. There is no limit to what may be thought or said, for all such ideas are but tokens of the experiences that people have had, are having, or would like to have. Thus it is that thought introduces an important new dimension to experience; it creates the worlds of might-have-been and is-to-be.

It is this new dimension that allows us to meddle in the normal flow of manifestation. It gives us the ability to anticipate events and encourage, prolong or forestall them by our actions. In this we have developed a powerful skill. Like all of our skills, it should not become a law unto itself but must be subordinated to the general well-being of the *whole* nature. No single faculty should be repressed, nor allowed a totally free rein. Through understanding we can bring our faculties into correct and harmonious relationship ready to serve our needs as we meet life and that which it brings to us.

Because the symbols and words that represent experience work like names we can use them to 'call' experiences. Our words and thoughts can, and in fact do, 're-call' the events they name. We can string our thoughts together in certain ways, assembling the forces of our inner dreamtime world and binding them together into a veritable army of creation that will act upon ourselves to change the way we interpret the events around us. Used in a certain way, thought has the power both to order experience and to produce experiences to order, the more so as thought and experience – name and thing – become closely associated: linked, but not confused.

Through thought we have the ability to call the forces behind experience into groups that will act upon ourselves and our surroundings in entirely new ways. We should, therefore, take care over *what* we think and *how* we think, practising the 'right thinking' of the Buddhists' eight-fold path.

Above all, if we are to make thoughts our co-workers rather than allowing them to oppress and enchain us, we will need to distinguish carefully between the thought and the experience. For thought gives us the ability to fabricate a representation of any experience whatsoever, and since we experience our thoughts then we can even think about thinking. We can talk about the thought-processes themselves, exactly as we are doing here, and this gives to thought the illusion of independent reality. Such representations of representations are fine for the purpose of discussions aimed at increasing our understanding, but we should be wary of acting towards those as though they were real in themselves, for hidden within this potentially infinite and circular process lie the gates of both sanity and pathology.

The Exercise

For the next session you are going to practise a type of meditation known as 'seed thought' meditation. The method here is to hold a particular thought or idea in mind so that it acts as a central seed or nucleus around which associated thoughts can gather.

You begin with the chosen seed thought and 'ponder' upon it. This will attract an associated thought or idea which you mentally note. This new thought may then give rise to a further associated thought which you note, again mentally. In this way you gather up a chain of linked ideas and thoughts firmly anchored at one end to the seed thought. Each new thought that arises is checked against the original seed idea and when you judge that the new thought is so far away from this original seed as to have no perceivable connection with it then you will discard that new thought. Return to the original seed thought and be ready to follow a new chain of ideas in some other direction.

Remember here that we are dealing with thoughts and ideas, not visual images. Of course, images may arise and may be noted, but they should be viewed as distractions from the meditating process.

Begin by making your opening gesture and relaxing, breathing rhythmically and deeply. Then take your chosen seed thought, dwelling upon it until an associated thought arises. If no other thoughts come up, turn your attention back to the original seed thought. If the thought that comes into your consciousness is followed by another additional association, you can accept this one too. The results you obtain will be one of the following:

(a) No thoughts come up.
    — Stick with the seed thought.
(b) One or two associated thoughts come up, with nothing more.
    — Return to the seed thought.
(c) A long chain of associated thoughts arise, leading further and further away from the seed thought.
    — When you assess that the latest thought is too far away from the original thought in association then return to the seed thought again.
(d) Complete loss of control of the meditation, going to sleep, daydreams, wild images, and so on.
    — Return to the seed thought.
(e) Something else entirely.
    — Return to the seed thought.

It is important at the end of this session that you write down the associations that came to mind. This is not a tremendous feat of memory. You will find it much easier than you might suspect to remember all the thoughts you have had in the session, for they have become linked together in chains through the meditation process itself and this makes them very easy to remember. Write them down in a notebook so that you will be able to refer back to them at a later time. This also serves to fix the associations in your mind, effectively transferring them to long-term memory.

Here is an example:

Date: 27/11/82   *Place:* Bedroom
Time: 7.00 a.m.
Seed: 'A Flame That Does Not Flicker'
Realizations: One must be as a flame that does not flicker on all levels. In the highest spiritual realm it is a display of the Divine Will. In the realm of

conscious thought it is the holding steady of an ideal. In terms of the emotions it is an independence of emotions, feeling what one will independent of the emotional atmosphere of the surroundings. In the physical world it would be the glow of health and light that is the firmness of the body to withstand disease. (*break*) A flame flickers normally when it is blown. Blown too hard it goes out. This flame does not register the winds of distractions. Therefore it does not flicker. This is how we should be.

Seed Thoughts

Some possible seed thoughts follow here. You should take two or three from this list, using each one for at least three sessions.

— The vast spiritual reservoir in which we live and move and have our being.

— Immutable rhythm is everywhere manifest in the universe.

— Pain occurs as a result of failing to adapt to change.

— Life is a bridge; cross over, but build no house thereon.

— There is no part of me that is not a part of the gods.

— No one throws stones at a barren tree.

— What appears to be truth is a wordly distortion of objective truth.

— The essence of truth is superior to the terminology of 'how' and 'why'.

— The teacher and the taught together produce the teaching.

— As waves come with the water and flames with fire, so the universal waves *with us*.

— The universe is an empty shell wherein mind frolics endlessly.

— Those who know others are wise; those who know themselves are enlightenend.

— The enlightened ones perform worldly duties conscientiously but are inwardly immersed in spiritual peace.

— The farther out one goes from the self, the less one knows.

— A high wind does not last all morning.

— When distinction is made between 'good' and 'bad', evil has already arisen.

— Man is the rescuer of matter.

— As I am lifted up I draw all unto me.

— The wise seek everything within, the ignorant from others.

— Man must *learn* to do what the hurricane, the whale, and the gnat do of their nature.
— This mind is not Buddha.
— A flame that does not flicker.
— A lamp has no rays at all in the face of the sun.
— He that loveth wisdom loveth Life, and they that seek her early shall be filled with joy.
— The path of the just is as the shining light, shining more and more unto the perfect day.
— Christ is our foundation and our chief cornerstone.
— The mind is the slayer of the real – slay the slayer!

Record your experiences in Table 4 before continuing further.

Table 4
Seed thoughts

Seed	Major realizations	Other experiences

Summary

— There are many ways of representing inner and outer experience.

— Effective representation relies on the *form* of the representation.

— Language, and therefore thought, have become the primary means of 'naming' experiences.

— Thoughts, like names, may call and gather together the things they represent.

— Thinking about thinking is both useful and dangerous.

— Practise the exercises and record your results *before* proceeding with the next chapter.

5
The Ocean of Emotion

Feedback

How did you enjoy the last session? Seed thought meditation really appeals to some people but not to others. Here for your comparison are some of the things that meditators have reported from their experiences with seed thought meditation.

— Some were all right but I had no success with others.
— I got into just repeating the seed thought over and over again in my head and did not get any associations.
— I had two or three thoughts in my mind and all was going fine. Then there was just a blank.
— It worked well for me. It brought into light material of different types; emotional, allegorical, pictorial.
— A lot of apparently unrelated ideas came up but I later saw that they were connected.
— I felt like I was going to leave my body.
— I had a sudden feeling of security and power all in one. An incredible experience.
— My associations kept coming to an end. Then I kept drifting off.
— Every time I came to the end of a chain I felt happy about it.
— I kept holding the seed thought in mind and the ideas seemed unrelated so I stayed with the seed thought and ignored everything else.
— I found novel combinations of ideas coming up – things that I had not thought of before and which were new to me.
— It seemed to work all right, but I did not understand.
— I think it would be useful to write them up as you go along.
— I gained several insights into myself.

— It was a bit active for me. I prefer a passive one.

— I found I could use it as a key to some part of myself to show what I was needing in life at that time.

— I kept getting into religious and philosophical discussions over the things that came up.

— I found that all my associations revolved around myself and my self image.

— I found that I kept wanting to follow the association chains to their logical conclusion rather than stick with the seed thought.

You have probably discovered for yourself now that thoughts have power to evoke emotional responses, and thereby bring about changes in yourself.

The Ocean of Emotion

We have seen that the forms used by us to represent our own experiences are distinct from the experiences themselves. We have seen that the name is not the thing. Thought responds to life in an abstract, descriptive way. The whole methodology of our Western scientific procedure is founded upon this idea, although such an approach is being challenged in more and more ways each day. Thought leads us to believe that we can become spectators of experience, standing back from reality and observing. Nothing could be further from the truth. We can never fully divorce ourselves from the situations we observe but must always take some part in them, acting upon them in the very process of observation itself.

In fact, the life force that works through us can never be anything other than a participator in the process of life itself. It is through our emotions that we become aware of this most strongly, for our emotions occur as reactions to our experiences. They are the responses that our own life energy makes to the situation in which it finds itself. They are transactions between life and life.

It is said that:

Sticks and stones
May break my bones
But words will never hurt me.

Whilst this is logically true, it says nothing of the way we may hurt ourselves. We take offence at allegations made about us and become angry. We are happy when praised without any thought as to whether such praise is justified or not. We become sad when chastised or condemned, and fearful when threatened. Here life is reacting to other representations of itself.

Life always seeks modes of expression whether we like it or not. If we will not become involved in the process of living directly we will be drawn into involvement with symbols – whether these be defined by ourselves, provided by others, or supplied by our own aberrant thought-processes.

The emotional life force is shared by us all. The same life that runs through you also runs through me. It runs throughout the whole of what Teilhard de Chardin called the 'biosphere'. Life is like the land itself, the body of the planet, for we all live upon it. Yet we can erect barriers, both actual and 'legal', to ensure our own unmolested use of a particular portion. In a similar way we claim ownership of some aspect of this one life force to which we wish to give expression. So much is this so that we become jealous of those who are too much like ourselves. A television producer of lively wit had occasion to work with one of the more famous comedians and told me later that this celebrity would in no way tolerate any other 'jokers' on the set beside himself. In some way we all have our special claim to a portion of the life force which we treat as exclusively our own domain. Yet wit calls forth wit, anger evokes anger, depression can bring us all down and enthusiasm can spread like a bush fire. Emotions cannot be anything but shared for they are the stuff of the life force itself.

Many mystics have referred to this shared life as 'love', for this expresses the way in which our own life force flows in another – 'co-inhering' as the mystic poet and novelist Charles Williams might have said. All our reactions then can be thought of as variations of this love – too much, too little, or wrongly directed. This system is completely worked out by Dante Alighieri in his *Divine Comedy*.

Elsewhere it has been said that all of our emotions can be reduced to combinations, in various degrees, of three basic ones. These are anger, happiness and sorrow – 'sad, glad, mad' as it is sometimes expressed – and this analysis taken from a modern system of psychotherapy matches well that expressed by the love mystics like Dante. These three emotions stem from the three basic ways that life can manifest, called power, love and wisdom by the occultists and often referred to as the three aspects or modes of operation of divinity. Under this system anger or energy is associated with the life force in its power aspect; joy or elation with the love aspect of life; and sadness or sorrow with life in its third aspect as wisdom, for the experiences that lead to wisdom pass first through the dark vale of tears.

These various ways that the life force behaves are of course not mutually exclusive but rather occur in combinations. If you are one of those who believe joy and sorrow to be exclusive of each other you should consider the emotions experienced at the start of a new phase of life where circumstances change dramatically, especially when those changes seem thrust upon you rather than to have been chosen of your own free will. At such times there is the joy of new beginnings mingled with the sadness for what has passed. The term 'bitter-sweet' expresses such feeling well, since there is always the opportunity for us to develop new ways of expressing our feelings and reactions to the events in our lives.

The one ocean of emotion flows through us all and the reactions of one person are easily communicated to others. This occurs in two ways. On the one hand, a strongly experienced emotion can bring about a similar one in other people. We see this working in the spread of emotion associated with religious experiences during ceremonial celebrations. Anger too can easily be whipped up and spread through a group of people, giving us the 'mob' effect. This is communication by similarity. There is, on the other hand, the possibility of communication by complement. In this case an aggressive emotion calls forth a sensation of submission in another person.

We can see how these operate by returning once more to the analogy of the land. Having erected artificial boundaries we thereby create the concepts of inclusion and exclusion. In this way, those who are 'with us', which is to say, by analogy, on the same piece of land, all experience expansion when we extend our boundaries. Those who are not 'with us' will, however, experience encroachment. Operating as groups or individuals we transmit by similarity or complement accordingly as we include or exclude the other within our own boundaries. This has far-reaching consequences for humanity in weal and woe.

Finally, when we take down our barriers, those in our immediate vicinity find that theirs have disappeared too. Without barriers we may all freely roam the land, keeping together or separate at will whilst yet holding all in common. At such a time we shall have entered the ocean of life experiencing the peaks and troughs of the waves that come to us, whether those waves are the products of natural forces or of human intervention.

The Exercise

For the next practice period you are going to work with sounds. These sounds can be imagined and heard internally or they can be sought out or produced as actual sounds in the world so that you may actually listen to them. In either case the method depends on becoming completely absorbed in the chosen sound, ignoring all other stimuli and distractions.

This style of meditation has at least two forms. The first is *mantra* meditation, in which a word, phrase or series of tones is repeated audibly or silently to oneself over and over again. The second type is *nadam* meditation, in which a natural and usually continuous sound is used. In fact any continuous sound may be used, as the list provided below indicates.

Over the next practice period, choose a mantra or nadam and stay with it for about five sessions. Then, if you wish, choose another sound. In the case of a mantra, you may intone it audibly or silently. In the case of a nadam, you may either imagine it or search out an external source for the sound. Relax and immerse yourself in the sounds, mentally noting as an aside any thoughts, images or feelings that occur. Retain your concentration throughout upon the sounds, returning calmly to them if you become distracted. At the end of the session, note your experiences in Table 5 so that you will be able to summarize them before proceeding further.

Mantra List
Here is a list of mantras which are drawn from many sources, cultures and languages. In some of the more obscure cases a translation into English is provided for information only. That is, the English version is not one of the mantras. Select the one which feels the most appropriate for you.

— OM (rhymes with 'home').
— OM Nama Shivaya.
— OM Mani Padme HUM.
— Nama Buddhaya Nama Dharmaya Nama Sanghaya.
— Ateh Gibur Le-olahm Adonai.
— La Ilaha Illa'llah.
— Visita Interiora Terrae Rectificando Invenies Occultum Lapidem.
— Qui Expansis In Cruce Manibus Traxisti Omnia Ad Te Secula.
— Hare Krishna Hare Krishna Krishna Krishna Hare Krishna.
— I am that soundless boundless bitter sea out of whose deeps life wells eternally.
— No number I shall not save
No depth I shall not cleanse
No breadth I shall not master
No height I shall not reach.

— I will go unto the altar of God even unto the God of my joy and gladness.
— Blessed be the Holy Trinity, the undivided Unity, Eternal Immortal Invisible, to Whom be all Honour and Glory for ever and ever amen.
— Oxoxma Plapli Iadnamad (Enochian – 'Make us partakers of the undefiled knowledge').
— Khabs Am Pekht (Egyptian – 'Light in extension').
— A Neba Sebebi Heh Unt-f Er T'etta Neb Nebu (Egyptian – 'Hail my Lord, Traversing Eternity, his existence being for ever and ever, Lord of Lords').
— A Sesu RA Ami-xet Ausar (Egyptian – 'Hail followers of Ra who are in the train of Osiris').

Nadam List
Here is a list of nadams from which you may select those most suited to your own nature and circumstances. You may extend the list if you wish. The important thing to keep in mind for this type of meditation is the essentially continuous nature of the sound. Use your imagination and improvise if necessary. When in the city you might try using the virtually incessant rumble of traffic as your nadam. Try not to judge the sound you are using, but become uncompromisingly involved in it.

— The hum of intoxicated bees.
— The vibration of an idling engine.
— Rainfall.
— Whistling sounds.
— High-frequency sounds.
— Waterfall.
— Roaring of an ocean.
— Sound of a bell ringing.
— Sound of a conch shell.
— Nasal, humming sound like that of a wire string.
— Sound of a small tight drum.
— Sound of a flute (bamboo).
— Echoing sound.
— Roll of distant thunder.

Table 5
Using sound

Sound chosen	Real/chanted or imagined	Summary of experiences

Other experiences

Summary

— Emotions are life reacting to life.
— The basic life force is shared by all in the biosphere.

— We can consider emotions to be made up of the three basics – mad, sad, glad.

— These are the three mystical aspects of divinity – power, wisdom and love – and these in turn may be seen as the various actions of love itself.

— Barriers control inclusion and exclusion and this determines whether we communicate our feelings by similarity or complement.

— Despite our artificial barriers, the life force is one and indivisible like the land and the ocean.

Practise the exercises and record your results as indicated *before* proceeding further.

6
Masks and Transformation

Feedback

I hope that you enjoyed the last session of mantra or nadam meditation. You should have noted a summary of your experiences with this meditation; if not, do so now, before proceeding with this chapter.

Here once again are some of the experiences that meditators have had with mantra or nadam exercises. These have been divided into two groups for a purpose which will be explained later.

Group A
— It quietened the thoughts.
— I think it's a good way to settle yourself down before doing another exercise.
— I found the mantra seemed too long.
— I seemed to keep my mind focused on the outside world.
— I found the whole thing too repetitive and boring.
— I didn't get anything. I stayed with the mantra but didn't get anything. It's just sounds, just sounds.
— I kept being distracted by my own thoughts.
— I found that the mantra helped quieten my body.
— It kept changing into something else.

Group B
— I started to get agitated and disturbed.
— I suddenly felt very sad during this session.
— I found that I could think without words whilst the mantra was going on.
— Whilst doing the mantra, I suddenly slipped into a whole community of people gathered under that mantra.

— Behind my mantra I found the birth of music and the birth of children.
— I had an experience of the language of the world with all its suffering.

As you can see, these two groups of experiences are quite different. See which type of experience more nearly describes your own. No doubt you will have had some experiences of one type and some of the other. You might find however, that you had experiences predominantly in one category.

These different experiences can help us decide whether a meditation style is suitable for us or not. The people who reported the experiences related in group A show signs of being distracted from their practice. We are very conservative creatures. Even the non-conformists amongst us are oppressed by their own established behaviour patterns and life values. Taking up meditation brings about changes in our natures and we unknowingly resist this. Often we resist that which we most desperately need. If you found the majority of your experiences to be like those in the first group, perhaps you might like to persevere with the method a little longer and see if any sort of 'breakthrough' occurs. This need not, of course, be the same as any of those listed under group B. It would, after all, be a sad thing to select only those practices which made us feel comfortable. This would be a sure sign that we were avoiding the challenge of real change and growth.

Masks and Transformation

William Shakespeare was one of many who have told us that the world in which we live is a stage and that we play many parts upon it. Not only is this true in terms of the different periods of development such as child, youth, adult and old age, but it also applies to us in an ongoing fashion during the course of our everyday life. We have different sets of behaviour patterns depending upon the situation we are in and the role we are playing. A shopkeeper may also be a mother, and a daughter. She may make and sell earthenware pots and chair the local citizens' action group. In each case there are different behaviours that are appropriate to each role, and these behaviours will define the way in which she walks and talks. They will decree which emotions may be expressed and which not.

A role is not something that we define for ourselves in isolation. Nor is it thrust upon us without our consent. These roles represent an agreed set of behavioural limits between ourselves and others that ideally remove unwanted or irrelevant patterns, leaving us free to get on with some transaction in undistracted absorption. As with so many other faculties, we have distorted this one too, oppressing each other with rigid role stereotypes, rather than expending the person-to-person investment of energy to define *dynamically* the edges of each role in our repertoire.

Beyond and behind all these roles is a very real aspect of our selves – the player or true self. This is the one that takes on all these roles, the one that *is* each one of these roles and much more besides. This true self willingly enters limitation in order to express more effectively some part of its extensive nature. Here is the purpose of set behavioural patterns. For they are like sets of clothes that are appropriate to certain activities. Many people use different sets of clothes for working, entertaining, relaxing, gardening, walking, swimming, and so on. They possess a richness in their varieties of expression available to their multi-faceted self. Yet others, lacking imagination, or attempting superficially to reject the use of roles entirely, show an unimpressive lack of variation. It is the very willingness to enter the limitation of a role that gives the rich, unfettered potential of the inner self its full expression.

Each role we take up provides us with an opportunity to fully develop and manifest a given aspect of our whole nature. A time will come, of course, for old roles to be discarded or re-defined, and new roles to be developed. As a certain aspect of self-development and growth becomes complete for us, the corresponding roles should drop away quite naturally, clearing the way for us to begin expressing some previously neglected part of our true self. These roles, however, should not be cast away too soon, for to do this would be to forgo the full expression of our true natures, thereby leading to incapacity or inadequacy in the face of life's later demands.

This advice is not popular with those who, irked by periodic restriction, want somehow just to 'be themselves'. In rejecting that which has a purpose beyond their understanding, they discard also the tools for achieving their ends. We can, however, come to identify ourselves too closely with our roles. We hold on to outmoded patterns, unwilling to find new ways of living which are more suitable to our evolving self for its expression in the world. When we are children, the things of childhood are most appropriate. But when we are adults, we must put aside the things of the child. A common example in Western society is that of the woman who has played the traditional mother role to her children. When she finally sees them grown and living their own lives, she may still cling to the mother role, desperately seeking other objects which will continue to define and fulfil for her that outmoded role. This can lead to feelings of failure, inadequacy and despair. Many people who have followed one particular career throughout their life suffer a crisis when they 'retire', regardless of the age at which they take this step. Again feelings of inadequacy – of being somehow left over, or surplus – can result, sapping the energy and undermining confidence in the future.

Feelings like this indicate to us that we are holding on to a role which is outdated or which does not suit the time and place. They indicate attachment to a role, and this shows a rigidity in reacting to life. For rather than picking a mask through which to view the world, we would do better to view the world first and then pick from our storehouse-repertoire the mask to suit the circumstances. It is therefore to our advantage to have as large a variety of masks as we can. It would also be helpful for us to choose more deliberately the role or mask according to need. But how to find first the central self behind the role, the player behind the mask? How do we find the central ideal that expresses our own perfection?

Different people become aware of their ideal self in different ways. For many it is experienced as a 'still small voice' within their deepest nature – beyond words, beyond thought, beyond feeling. No words can wholly capture this formless experience of the reality of the inner self. For others it is simpler to see that inner perfection in external principles – or in ideal people – and so these find it appropriate to take some religious leader as representing to them their own ideal of a perfected person. The leader chosen, whether it be Christ, Buddha, a personal guru, or whatever else, acts then as a mirror to the devotee of their own self-in-the-making. When we find for ourselves those spiritual values and people that 'strike a chord' in our own hearts, we soon feel their magnetizing effect. We want nothing more in life than simply to be like them. Slowly but surely our nature begins to turn in a new direction, and we become 'converted'. All the various and multifarious aspects of our life gather together around that one centre which gives them cohesion and meaning, allowing superficial affectations to drop away. We have found our centre.

The Exercise

The meditation exercise that you are going to undertake for the next practice period is in two parts and you should complete the first part before attempting the second part. This is important. The ideas that you will need for the second part of the practice must be obtained by performing the first part.

Part One
At the regular time which you have put aside for your practice, open your session and begin relaxing, allowing the breath to become regular and deep. Bring the power of your thoughts together into a state of poised readiness.

When you feel quite ready, bring every faculty and skill to bear upon consideration of this one thought: WHO AM I? Ask yourself this question. Let it mull over and over in your mind, permeating every part of your being. In fact, you should also turn loose the faculties of which you are not normally aware on this problem by keeping this question – WHO AM I? – in mind as you fall asleep at night.

At some point in your practice, whether immediately or only after many sessions, you will be struck either by some thought representing a high religious ideal or by a strong impression of one of the world's religious or spiritual teachers, real or legendary. This response to your probing meditation will have an unmistakable quality of immediate truth, heightened reality, a powerful sense of presence, a sudden expansion of consciousness as when you 'get' a joke, or some similar notable accompanying experience. You should continue your practice until you have this experience, and you must accept the *first* response of this type that you receive. It may not be an ideal or person that you would have chosen for yourself in the normal way. In fact, it probably will *not* be. Yet there is in almost every case a sense of the 'rightness' of that which emerges. Once having achieved this response, you are ready to proceed with the second part of the exercise.

Part Two

For this practice it is not necessary to use the previous system of opening gesture, relaxation, regular time and so on. Of course, you may retain these if you wish. At least once each day you must turn your attention to that ideal or person which was the centre of the response you received during the first part of the practice. You should get as much feeling and dedication into this exercise as possible. The idea is to practise some form of devotion to your ideal, attempting to 'lift your heart' towards that spiritual height.

The form that this devotion takes is purely personal and should be devised by your own ingenuity. One method is to make a small 'shrine' for your ideal. It does not have to be an elaborate affair, as its main purpose is to provide a focusing point for your aspirations, thereby acting rather like a lens to concentrate your intention. This shrine could be daily decorated with flowers from the garden. Or perhaps you would prefer to offer food prior to eating it. You might feel more comfortable telling your 'news' each evening, asking advice and communicating by using your heart rather than your head. Whatever method you devise, the idea is to raise the whole level of your thoughts, feelings and aspirations towards the ideal self as epitomized in the symbolic form you have discovered, making that symbol as real and as much a part of your life as possible.

A further complementary practice should also be brought into operation each day. Take some task of your normal life, whether it be in your employment, at home, in a social setting or practising a hobby, and perform that task as though its results were an offering to your spiritual principle. In every way that you can, dedicate yourself and your works to your ideal, for this ideal came to you in response to the search for your own true self. Whilst you may not see this self directly, you may very well be able to see it reflected in one of our world teachers, or in the tenets of the highest ideals that have been brought to us by such teachers. Try throughout the period to become more aware of the operation of the ideal in your own life and to encourage your own dedication and devotion to it.

Write up a summary of your experiences in Table 6 before proceeding further.

Table 6
The Ideal Self

My ideal is:

Realizations whilst practising devotions

Summary

— We play many parts, or roles, each day of our lives.
— Behind them all is the player, the true self.
— The self can willingly and knowingly enter the limitations of a role in order to develop some aspect of itself.

— We can become attached to roles, identifying with them. This holding on to outmoded patterns of behaviour leads to feelings of inadequacy and frustration.

— Each role seeks to express an aspect of our true self. This true self is our ideal and we can become aware of it by means of its reflection in the great teachers and religious leaders or in their teachings.

— Devotion to these ideals centres us and harmonizes all our various roles, thereby effecting an integration of the self.

— Practise these exercises and record your results *before* proceeding further.

7
The Place of Power

Feedback

Over the last practice period, we have been doing a slightly different form of meditation, a form which is sometimes called contemplation. It is regarded by some commentators and practitioners as a 'higher form' of meditation. I hope that you had some rewarding experiences with these exercises, which, after all, were designed to stimulate and awaken yet another faculty of your nature.

Here are some of the experiences that meditators have encountered with this particular exercise.

— It gave me a contact for meditation but it was very difficult to carry it through.
— I'd been doing this for years and not knowing it was meditation and suddenly it clicked.
— The mental atmosphere is much more critical in this form of meditation than in the others.
— It all depends on your own nature whether you are devotionally inclined or not. I already knew what way to go. I didn't set aside a particular time but drew upon the central quality in everyday life through a sort of 'presence' epitomized by the figure that came to me.
— I found it a useful experience.

The problem in recording people's experiences here is due to the intensely personal nature of those experiences. If you had any success with this particular form of meditation, you will have experienced a close personal link with an ideal or a great teacher, and with that link a feeling of love, security and warmth. Remember at all times, though, that this is your own divine nature being reflected back to you by such a teacher, for it is the task of such to awaken each one of us to the reality of the divine hidden deep within us.

If you have not had these experiences, do not despair or feel that you have missed something, for different meditation practices suit different people. It may be that a form of expression suitable for one person just will not work for another. The exercises here are provided so that between them, they will bring benefit to the widest range of people. The way of the devotional mystic is only suited to some, not all.

The Place of Power

Humanity stands between two realms of being, bridging the very large and the very small. We exist midway, it seems, between the tiniest, abstractly existing, sub-nuclear particles and the vast galactic processes far beyond our tiny planet. At both extremes we have found sources of almost inconceivable power. In the tiniest portion of matter is locked a vast storehouse of energy which can be unleashed in either the service or destruction of our race. The cosmos itself is like a huge factory in which the stars and the galaxies themselves are whirling in an ongoing dance of creation, change and destruction.

These vast forces operate without thought as we know it. They have no values, no conceptions of right and wrong. They operate in a totally impersonal fashion, taking no account of the scale of life within which we normally live. Unlike them, we mortals have the power to choose, and also to use. Our skills in controlling and manipulating nuclear and cosmic forces increase almost daily. It has been said that power corrupts and absolute power corrupts absolutely. Yet the human race is gaining access to forces and powers of ever greater intensities and potential. What are we to make of such power without a corresponding ethic? How are we to control the powers that exist around us if we cannot properly channel those that flow within our own personalities? Where greater Power is available it should be balanced by an access to greater Wisdom and, more importantly, greater Love, for love is that which stands behind all.

We can work with energy, at all levels of application, in a number of ways. We can transfer one type of energy to another. An electric heater converts electrical energy to heat energy. We can bind energy into a solid form as in the production of isotopes. Or we can release the energy contained within a form by breaking down that form, as in the simple and age-old process of lighting a fire. These, however, all amount to the same thing, for matter is 'locked up' energy and energy is 'released' matter. In dealing with these forces we influence some energy or matter that is of its own nature amoral, and we direct it to our own ends. In this sense, matter is essentially 'innocent'. This is quite the opposite idea to that held by those who commit the Manichaean heresy, claiming that matter is 'evil' and 'fallen'. On the contrary, matter in its own nature is still pure and unsullied, and remains so but for the uses to which it is put by the human race. It is we who have lost our innocence and brought down all the rest of creation thereby. And it is we who can rescue that fallen creation through the use of love.

Let us then never bind energy into a solid form except we do it with love. Energy transformations exist on many levels beside the apparently physical. One method, for example, of binding energy into a solid form is to bring together a number of people to work upon a common project. Energy so contained and directed in upon itself gives rise to manifestation. Let us always do this with love as the motive, whether building a house, or a computer system, teaching a course or planning a holiday.

Let us also never release energy except it too be done in love, for to release energy is to destroy the form in which it manifested. The birth of energy implies the death of the form which it previously held. Whilst many of us are hidebound in our prejudices and would dearly desire to be set free of such bondage, we would not welcome the destruction of our cherished and outmoded forms unless it were done with love for us.

Though we are flanked by awesome powers within the infinitely large and the infinitely small, we yet do have our own version of power. Far from being puny creatures at the mercy of the elements, we have a power which can all but destroy the whole of creation. We have the power to choose. We have, in fact, the power to do exactly as we wish, within whatever bonds constrain us from time to time. We are able to use or not use every single faculty we possess at any time unless we are forcibly restrained or compelled with respect to that faculty. To exercise our choice in the face of dire circumstances may certainly lead to death or injury. Yet the fact remains that the choice is always there and it is always we who make it. We should then choose with the motive of love.

What is love? One of the most frequently asked questions of all time. There is more to love, as the idea is used here, than the mundane kind that may exist between two people as we usually perceive it, although this is one of its manifestations. Love as it is used here means a vital concern for all other people, all other life. It is the recognition that each person is, like ourselves, an aspect of their own ideal self, a living acknowledgement that deep within we all share the same divinity. This love crosses the boundaries between people, between species, and between different realms of being. It transcends difference, seeking only a similar caring self.

By practising meditation we are led to a more integrated and whole self. This results in the destruction or conversion of many behaviour processes that normally cramp our ability to live fully. With this release, there comes an increase in personal power and energy. It is therefore of paramount importance that those who seek to increase and apply their knowledge of the self, should make those powers subservient to love. We can fool ourselves with this, of course. We can use the war cry 'for your own good'. On analysis this often turns out to be more aptly described as 'for *my* own comfort'. One of the more blatant examples of this is that of the interrogator who hammered a wooden wedge into the mouth of a burning martyr lest he jeopardize his soul by uttering heresies. Under such a travesty of transpersonal love we may perpetrate all manner of atrocities. Love binds as much as it severs or banishes.

No debate as to whether means justify ends or vice versa will guide us through the fog within which the wielding of power enfolds us. Quite simply such discussion misses the point. Both means and ends are irrelevant to any investigation of 'should'. Love and faulty technique is far superior to loveless precision. This applies equally to all energy matters, from cooking a meal to bringing up children.

In unfolding our powers, and especially the power of choice in ourselves, there is a spiritual ethic which becomes ever more important. This ethic applies equally to all forms of life – including yourself. Quite simply it states: 'Love all, harm none, do what you will.'

The Exercise

The meditation presented here is for many reasons not so widely known as the other types which you have been practising. It is called *mudra* meditation and is the meditation of movement.

Movement is of course embodied in certain sequences of hatha yoga posture and its value has been recognized in the West in the studies of body awareness and body language on the one hand and the states of mind induced by running and jogging on the other. It finds its fullest expression, however, in the Chinese exercise known as T'ai-Chi Ch'uan or 'supreme ultimate boxing'. This gentle art includes an exercise of flowing movements that brings tranquillity to the minds of its practitioners.

The essence of mudra meditation is to absorb your whole being and awareness into the movements you make with your body. The methods are very straightforward. You do not have to be an athlete to perform these meditations. Three examples are given here and you may try one, two or all three over the practice session. Try to become silent within and lose yourself in the movements that you make. Try to think of nothing but the movements you are using.

Mudra 1
This mudra is taken from Indian sources. Sit comfortably, resting the back of your hands on your thighs or knees so that the palms are uppermost, arms quite relaxed. Breath out. On breathing in, touch the thumb tip to each of the fingertips in turn, starting with the first or index finger and ending with the little finger. Relax the hand and breath out. The cycle then begins again. Take care to synchronize the movements of the left and right hands. These movements should be flowing, almost dance-like, with the hands as relaxed as possible. The breathing should be slow, deep and relaxed and the whole action almost without thought, such is your degree of absorption with it. For the duration of the meditation session, nothing exists for you but the action you are performing.

Mudra 2
This one is a little more energetic. It is taken from a Western version of an oriental 'life-prolonging' exercise. It is called the stretch mudra. Stand with your feet apart the distance between your shoulders. Stand in a relaxed way, quietening the thoughts whilst breathing deeply and rhythmically. On an in-breath, slowly raise your right hand, palm down, forwards and upwards, until it is straight up above your head. As you raise your arm, filling your lungs with air, you also rise up on your toes, until you are stretching slightly. Hold this position and the breath for just a moment. Slowly lower the arm in an arc to the side this time whilst exhaling. At the same time gradually come off your toes, so that you are standing normally again by the time your arm is at your side and your lungs are empty. Pause for a moment before continuing.

The next part of the cycle is a repeat of the first part, but using the left arm this time. Then the final part is a further repeat of the action using both arms together. This completes the cycle, as shown in Figure 6, which then begins again with the first part. Try to co-ordinate exactly the arm and ankle movements with the breath. Keep your attention on the movements themselves, performing them all in a relaxed and graceful fashion without effort or strain.

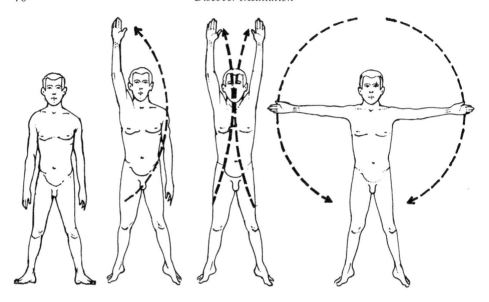

Figure 6
The Stretch

Mudra 3

The third mudra is based upon the posture 'Wave hands in clouds' in the solo exercise of T'ai-Chi Ch'uan. The movements are shown in Figure 7.

Take up a relaxed stance with your feet apart the distance between your shoulders. Breathe in a relaxed and deep rhythm. Slowly and calmly move into the starting position by swinging your left hand, palm upwards, to the right hip and raising the right hand palm downwards to the right ear. At the same time, shift your weight completely onto your right leg, turn your body slightly to the right, and turn your head to look right. Breathing in, move gracefully into the opposite position by gradually shifting your weight onto your left leg whilst turning your head and body leftwards, pivoting at the waist. As you do this the upper hand moves downwards close to the body, palm inwards and the lower arm rises on the outside, palm to the body. At the half-way point of the movement the weight is momentarily evenly distributed between the two feet. The hands are at the same level in front of the body, the closer one falling and the further one rising. The head and body are facing the front.

On reaching the second position, pause and breathe out. On the next in-breath, shift the weight to the right leg once more, moving the hands and body

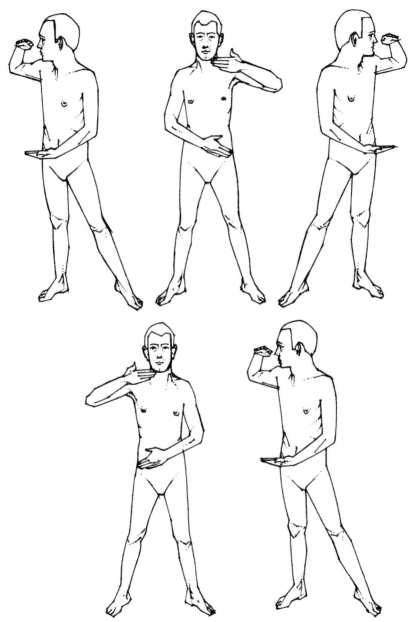

Figure 7
Wave hands in clouds

as before to take up the first position again. This time, however, it is the left hand that passes closest to the body. Pause here once more whilst breathing out. This completes the cycle which may now be repeated. Make the movements relaxed and graceful with weight change, body timing and hand movements all co-ordinated into one flow. Let the head and eyes follow the movement of the hands.

As usual, note down your experience, in Table 7, before proceeding further.

Table 7
Meditation of movement

Mudra used	Experiences
1	
2	
3	

Special experiences

Summary

— Humanity stands half-way between two realms of awesome power.
— Our power lies in our ability to choose, to will.
— We can manipulate the essentially innocent forces of nature, bringing them down to our own deviated level or raising all consciousness generally, depending on our ethic.
— As we practise meditation we release our own energies and those too can be used in different ways according to our ethic.
— This ethic for the use of power, especially the power to choose, is that of love.
— Love is a bridge across all boundaries, whether between people or between species, or even between different modes of existence. It is applied in the mystical tenet: 'Love all, harm none, do what you will.'
— Practise the exercises and record your results *before* proceeding further.

8
Quests and Questers

Feedback

Now compare your experiences with those recorded by others who have practised these exercises.

— The first one was OK. I couldn't do the others.
— I kept getting a double-image feeling in my hands. They felt in two places at once.
— I felt like a guide showing the way.
— It made me feel like a tree with branches.
— I kept seeing all different sorts of colours and shapes.
— I felt like I was rocking a baby.
— I felt as though I was turning round at the same time I was doing it.
— It made me think of the symbolism of the cross.
— I spend the whole time working on precision of movement. I got bored with it, did it fast and got giddy.
— I felt silly doing it, so gave it up.
— I got a lot more out of other exercises than this one. I don't think this is meditation.
— I felt suddenly that the exercise was 'doing me', rather than vice versa.

You will of course have had your own individual experience with this exercise. Sometimes things are not noticed or recorded until the attention is drawn to them. The experience of tingling in the hands or a feeling of warmth coursing through the body are two such experiences. Perhaps you have had these experiences or similar physical symptoms. If so, record them now.

Bringing awareness totally into our actions as we perform them diverts us from blocking the normal flow of the life force within us. This sudden release of a greater flow of life through our being brings vitality and warmth in its wake. It is just this increased flow of vitality that is responsible for many of these mudra forms being classified as health-giving exercises. They are indeed essentially beneficial, whether simply releasing the life force itself by distracting our normal thinking process away from its habitual blocking of that energy, or as in the more sophisticated forms of exercise, the movements themselves channelling that energy along the meridians and energy channels of our subtle nature.

Quests and Questers

All who undertake meditation practices and systems of spiritual development find themselves engaged upon a quest as profound as that followed by the famous Knights of the Round Table. When examining the motives behind our need to practise some form of meditation we usually find a deep-seated desire for self-knowledge and self-fulfilment. We want to be able to throw additional light on the obscure areas of the self, dispelling the gloom that lurks therein.

But what is it all for? Why are we driven to do these things? Do we merely follow the blind thrust of life, like the seed which sprouts from the ground, groping from the darkness towards the sun? On the contrary, for the practice of meditational techniques enables us to take a more active part in determining our growth and in encouraging our own inner unfolding. We gradually pass through various stages of self-knowledge brought about by exercises such as these which turn the attention inwards. We become increasingly aware of the world around us and our own responsibility for the glee or gloom we experience there. We begin to see that certain, to us undesirable, circumstances continually come about as a result of some aspect of our own selves. We come to realize that here lie the keys to the changes we must make in ourselves to modify our existence and bring it into one accord with the values and ideals which we hold dear.

This is no easy task. It requires constant vigilance and unwavering dedication. Yet this very effort enables us to develop the skills which eliminate that which is destructive and enhance that which is beneficial. It is these qualities of character, built step by step, that bring us to the point where we become true monarchs of our own inner realms. We gain in skill and ability, in power and knowledge and, because of the trials we must go through to effect these changes in our stubborn selves, we gain in love and understanding too.

Traditionally, monarchs were the protectors as well as the leaders of their people and in this sense they were regarded spiritually as the servants of their subjects. History abounds, sadly, with examples of those who sought only to rule as masters, wielding tyrannical oppression over their subordinates. At one time the rulers, whether monarchs or priests and priestesses, held their position by virtue of their superiority in some particular quality. These qualities are generally variations on the three basic aspects of power, love and wisdom. Over the centuries, in various periods of history, the rulers came to be chosen by line of succession, usually patrilineal. Clearly such a monarch would have a high degree of development in the essential virtues only by accident, if at all, unless the traditional methods of spiritual training were retained – which generally they were not. This leads logically to the situation we have today in the various forms of democracy and 'people-based' government systems. The service once performed *for* us has been given back so that we must now determine direction for ourselves and also protect ourselves. We clearly must go through this stage in our development, but it has brought many ills and injustices into the world.

You, however, will reach that stage where you become monarch of your own self and, therefore, a servant of others. Now it is ridiculous to suppose wise monarchs would place their own wisdom below that of their people. It is nonsense to suppose that a monarch would place hard-won spiritual qualities at the indiscriminate use of those who have chosen to remain in the warmth and comfort of relative ignorance. Being a servant in this respect does not mean being 'ordered about'. In fact, in earlier times a slave who had to be given instructions all the time was considered worse than useless – a fact overlooked by many tyrannical managers and parents in our present day. To be of service, we must use our powers, skills and qualities in the way which we alone see fit regardless of the demands of others. Yet we should exercise those abilities in the service of others who do not possess them.

Armies used to be raised to protect the people of an area, and these consisted of men who undertook special and rigorous training. At the culmination of their development they used their skills on behalf of those who did not possess them. We should follow the same rule ourselves, whether acting with power, as in this example, or with love, or with wisdom. We can make our qualities available when they are lacking in a needy situation.

All the cells of our bodies are of the same basic structure. Yet most have specialized to fulfil certain functions. These perform faithfully according to type in proper relationship with their neighbours; and are we not all similar cells of this planet's biosphere? Do we not each have our own individual nature despite similarity of structure? We each specialize and, having become unique, we should then use our speciality in correct relationship to the whole. To do otherwise is to introduce a cancerous growth into the living body of life on this planet. We emerge as individuals purely because we have a part to play. It is to be played by us alone, on behalf of the whole, and not by others who have their own tasks to do.

Like the armies of old, the recruits of the mystery schools learn their skills so that they may be used on behalf of those who do not have them. One of the titles of the Pope, by the way, is 'Servant of the servants of God' and quite apart from the views you may have about this person in particular or Catholicism in general, the title is an apt description of a proper attitude. A present-day teacher of meditation techniques in an international occult school was asked what made him take up teaching. He replied that it was the only way he knew even to begin to repay all that his teacher had done for him. Not everyone becomes a teacher, but at that stage of your development where those who guide you say: 'I can do no more for you. You are now in charge of yourself,' you become a monarch of your own self.

From this point you take on the responsibility of applying your own self in the service of others. In this way you will come to the realization that, in the words of a Middle-Eastern saying, only those who know how to follow are true leaders.

The Exercise

We now come to a type of meditation which has been popularized as a psychological technique in recent times. It is most often referred to as the method of fantasy journey and it works by the use of the creative imagination to build a story in which you take part. It is like an active and intentional daydream, a daydream under control and following a set pattern. Almost anything that you imagine or play through in your mind is a fantasy journey and whereas some of these are suitable for training in spiritual development others are only useful for psychological insights because they do not reach to the deep inner levels of unawareness. The difference between these types is the degree to which the journey is constructed along archetypal principles, those enduring principles which occur again and again in myths and legends of all times and across many cultures. There are varying degrees of this, of course. You can imagine a progression of symbols, from those which are purely personal and not shared by anyone else, to those which are common to the people of your time and culture. The further we go the more we see similarities between these symbols and more general and more powerful ones that stand behind the purely transitory and temporal.

Those fantasy journeys which are carefully and deliberately constructed to pierce deep into the inner realms are usually called pathworkings. They have been used as training devices in the mystery traditions and schools for literally thousands of years. Over the next period of practice, you will follow the pathworking given here. The method is simplicity itself. You should either read through the description of the pathworking sufficient times to memorize it in detail or, alternatively, you should read the pathworking into a tape recorder, allowing pauses where indicated by dots, and speaking slowly enough for you later to be able to build the images described in comfortable time. Having done this you should relax in a place where you will not be disturbed and begin building the images in the mind's eye according to your memory or the tape recorder – your memory's external aid.

The important thing to remember about these pathworkings is that everything that you encounter is your own construction. If you ignore this you will be led sadly astray. For though you follow as carefully as possible the descriptions given, you will find sometimes that other elements enter the pathworking unbidden. In such cases you should note that this happened and, providing the context of the pathworking is not altered thereby, you may accept what you have seen or understood in the pathworking. Sometimes, however, such images or thoughts that arise attract you away from the pathworking itself. If this occurs, they should be ignored and the pathworking continued. You should treat a pathworking exactly as you would treat a journey on foot in the normal world. For example, if you were on your way to a certain place and whilst walking met someone who invited you to go in a completely different direction, you would have no trouble in knowing how to deal with this situation, and you would probably politely refuse, indicating your intended purpose. There is no difference in these workings of the imagination. However, keep in mind that every vision, every thought, every entity that you encounter is produced by you. It may be that it represents a reality other than yourself, but the symbolic form that you encounter is produced by you alone and does not necessarily match the real form of any other being.

The particular pathworking given here is designed to bring you in touch with your inner guide. The inner guide is a principle within yourself which acts like a spiritual compass. It is that part of you which knows what to do, what direction you should take for your own proper development. It is through this faculty that you are drawn to and recognize the teachings of others.

Like all forms met in these pathworkings, the inner guide figure is a principle that connects you and *not*-you. The actual form in which the guide appears is derived from your own imagination, your memory or by construction. The principle represented is a part of your own nature outside your awareness. You also share many of these principles, especially that of the inner guide, with countless other people. In this sense the principle is also transpersonal and archetypal, representing an external force or entity.

The exercise should be performed as many times as necessary for the guide contact to occur. This may be on the first session and it may not. The important point is to build all the images up to the actual meeting point and then *wait* momentarily. There should be a feeling of warmth, love and caring from the guide figure. If this is not present, then your image is a false guide. The emotions need not be an overpowering sensation. But if it is totally absent the chances are that you have 'made up' the guide and you will have to do the working again at another time. These false guides represent ego-projections and they should be deliberately absorbed back into yourself, prior to leaving the working by the door behind you as described in the working itself.

Once you have obtained your contact you should ask for instructions as to how you should enter and leave this world of imagination and how you are to re-establish contact with your guide again. The method given to you at that time will be purely personal. Your guide may be happy for the time being for you to use the same pathworking each time you wish to meet. On the other hand you may be shown a door that you may use. You might be invited to the guide's 'cottage' or to some other setting that will form the basis of your later meetings. Follow the instructions carefully and write them down as soon as you can after the session. Pathworkings are often 'keyed' with their own image which appears as a design upon a door. The design for this working is of the sun rising behind a high mountain.

Here then is the description of the pathworking. It is called 'The Dark Wood' and is used as an introduction to a series of pathworkings exploring different parts of the inner realms.

The Dark Wood
Come with me now upon a journey . . . a journey deep within, to that inner realm that is the source of all Light, all Life, all Love . . .

You stand before a door, the door between the worlds. Let this image arise in your mind's eye clearly and distinctly, as with all the images on this journey.

Upon this door is a design. Examine it closely . . .

Figure 8
Door design for pathworking 'The Dark Wood'

Then open the door and step through into a grey, swirling mist . . .

The door closes behind you and you see that on this side too it bears the same design. This will be your door back to consciousness at the end of the working. At that time it will appear behind you wherever you are. It will also appear if you wish for any reason to leave this working part-way through. At any time that you wish, you have only to turn around and call upon this door for it to appear, giving you access back to normal consciousness.

The door fades into the mist . . . There is no sense of up or down, forward or back . . . You are just floating, floating . . .

It begins to get darker as the mist begins to clear and swirls windlessly away . . . It is night, a night dark and black . . . As you peer into the gloom you begin to make out the shapes of trees . . . You are in a wood or forest of some sort and it is night, dark and moonless . . . The door is gone. Was there ever a door? . . . Is that really how you entered this wood? . . . Perhaps it was your imagination . . . There are only dark brooding trees on every side . . . You have been here a very, very, long time . . . Darkness on all sides . . . You no longer remember how you stumbled into this wood . . . Try to think. How did you get here? What are you doing *here*?

You are hopelessly lost . . . Yet you must get back onto the track somehow . . . You are sure there was a track, once upon a time . . . You look around . . . Every direction seems equally hopeless, equally menacing . . . Still, there has to be a way out, and you might find it if you keep awake to yourself this time.

You strike out in one direction at random, pushing through the undergrowth and tree branches . . . It is hard going . . . You push on as best you can . . .

After a while you notice it is easier to go in some directions than others . . . Sometimes you fight with vines and tendrils, whilst at other times they almost part for you . . . Surely this easy way is how you stumbled into this wood in the first place . . . Stop for a moment, for here is your clue . . . If you entered this lightless realm by following the paths of least resistance, then your way back must be to retrace your steps in the opposite direction . . . You turn and push into the resistance of the undergrowth . . . You welcome this resistance for it shows you are on the right track . . . On and on you go . . . Pushing and struggling through the wood . . . Is that a clearing ahead ? . . . You head for the point where the trees seem thinnest . . . You push through a last tangle of branches and emerge into the open . . .

It is still dark but you can make out a narrow track that continues off, leading up a hill, high and steep, a dark outline against the rapidly lightening sky . . . The edge of the wood is behind you and extends in each direction for as far as you can see . . . You look at your surroundings, which are becoming lighter moment by moment . . . You look against the hill's peak and are suddenly dazzled by the sun rising from behind it . . . Its rays flash out in a cross shape, turning the peak of the hill golden pink . . . Here at last is the place you were seeking . . . There is your goal ahead upon that far peak . . . Tears of joy well up in your eyes . . . No more lost wanderings . . . No more pain and suffering . . . Here it is before you . . . Here is your goal . . .

It looks a long climb . . . But the day is early, so you rest just for a moment and gather your strength . . . Don't want to overdo it . . . Better make all the preparations first . . . That wood looks cool and inviting . . .

No. Enough of this. 'What are you waiting for? . . . You set off upon your joyful climb . . . It is so easy to be distracted . . . But not any more . . . You are going to keep your eye on that peak and go straight up this time . . .

Straight up, you begin your ascent . . . It gets steeper and steeper as you go . . . Soon you lose sight of the peak due to the hill's curvature . . . Still, as long as you keep heading upwards on this track you should reach the peak all right . . .

Something ahead catches your eye . . . A leopard is crossing and recrossing the track, working downwards . . . It comes closer as you watch . . . It is not fierce . . . It is as playful as a kitten . . . It turns and turns again, weaving across the path in front of you . . . Each time you try to step forward, it somehow gets under your feet, preventing you from continuing . . . It hinders you . . . It forces you to drop back down the track again . . . What to do?. . . What to do?. . .

You drop back and leave the track . . . Perhaps you can skirt around this hindrance . . . You continue to the side, not going upward, but not going downward either . . . You have already lost a lot of ground . . . Still, there is plenty of time yet to reach the peak before nightfall . . . Even with no track now, you can still tell which way to go by the slope of the ground . . .

You strike out up the slope again . . . Immediately, a lion appears from nowhere . . . It bars your way fiercely . . . It is huge . . . Such savagery stops you cold . . . Have you the courage to confront it?. . . It rears menacingly . . . Then the leopard too joins it . . . It frolics to and fro to prevent you from skirting around the lion . . . The only way you can go is down . . . Courage now . . . Stand your ground . . .

Beyond the lion, there appears a wolf, lean and hungry, foam-jawed . . . A wave of dark evil and malevolence washes over you . . . You seem to see again the bright flash of the hill's peak, as the animals crowd towards you, pushing, snarling and slavering . . .

Herded and threatened, you drop back . . . So near, yet an eternity away . . . Such a deep loss of so bright a promise . . . You are being pushed downwards and back to the dark wood . . . You feel the loss keenly . . . Tears sting your eyes as hope dies . . . Further and further away the animals herd you . . . You cannot stand against their combined force . . . Closer and closer you are pushed towards the lost realm . . . Despair. To have been so close. To have awoken. To have had the vision and then lost it . . . You stumble to face that forest of gloom . . . On the right stands a man, robed and hooded . . . You cry out for help . . . From the depths of despair you call to him . . . He hears . . . He comes to your side . . . The animals draw back a little . . . (pause . . .)

The man asks why you have turned back from your quest . . . You indicate the animals barring your way . . . He explains that the straight, steep road is the way of the great saints . . . He says that there is another way . . . It is longer but easier, yet it has its share of perils . . . He offers to show you the way which, though dark at first, leads through torment to where there is acceptance . . . He can lead you to the Loved One . . . the One who can lead you into bliss . . .

Can you trust him? Is it safe to go with him? How did he come to be here?. . . You ask him . . .

He replies that he was sent by the Loved One and in that name comes specifically to aid you, ready to guide you to your goal . . .

Think now. Can you do it?. . . Maybe it's too much to ask . . . Why *you* anyway?. . . What's so special about *you*?. . . Who do you think you are, anyway?. . . You already did very badly on your first try. What if you should start off and then fail miserably again?. . .

Your guide answers. You dither out of fear and fear alone. It is *love* that singles you out, as it does all who take these paths . . . It is through the medium of love that your guide now appears . . . Whatever is the object of your heart's love and devotion, this now seeks you out and, through the mediation of your guide, draws you ever closer.

Come . . . Follow . . .

You follow your guide . . . Here your guide explains to you how you will come and go between the realms and what signs and symbols, for the moment, you will use. When you have seen the doors and suchlike and heard all your instructions it will be time for you to leave. You will then locate behind you the door by which you first entered this working and, with a farewell to your guide, step through into normal consciousness, closing the door firmly behind you. But for the moment, listen to your guide . . .

Write down your experiences in Table 8.

Table 8
Pathworking experiences

General realizations

Impressions of the guide

Instructions received

Summary

— We have a deep-seated need for self-knowledge and self-unfolding.

— As we achieve this we become more in control of ourselves at all levels, through working upon our own natures to remove deviations and that which brings suffering.

— We become monarchs of ourselves, yet a monarch is as much a servant as a leader.

— Great skills can be ours because we are unique individuals. Yet, like the cells of the body, we should use our uniqueness in the service of those who lack our skills.

— Practise the exercise and record your results *before* proceeding further.

9
Reality

Feedback

Well, how did you do in that last session? Did you make contact with a guide? If you did not and gave up, don't despair, for it merely means that this type of meditation is not suitable for your use. Like all of the forms presented in this manual, it may suit some people but not others. It is presented so that you may have an opportunity of trying it out and forming your own assessment of its uses and benefits. Such assessment will be soundly based upon your direct experience of its effects, rather than on the abstract descriptions of an academic commentary upon the method.

If, however, you did make contact with the guide figure and you feel that you would like to pursue this style of meditation, then you should consult Appendix B at the end of this book for further information.

If you are ever in doubt about which particular spiritual methods and systems to use, then relax, close your eyes and ask your guide!

Reality

It would be very easy for us to retreat from the world around us, claiming to follow a path of spiritual development. But in the last analysis, our reality consists of the contents of our awareness. For most of our lives that awareness is directed to what we think of as the outside world. No matter what experiences we may have with meditation, what great realizations we may uncover, what deep insights into our characters and ourselves we may achieve, none of these become truly real unless and until changes occur in the world around us.

In many legends a folk hero descends into the underworld or death-world and returns bringing goods of value to his people. In other words, the experiences found within are translated into tangible effects in the outside world, for remember it is this that is our mirror, reflecting back to us our inner nature. All the practices and techniques we use are empty and void of meaning if they do not bring about changes in the world. So, it is all very well to develop our spiritual faculties, but when we finish our meditation sessions, we are then back in the world again, carrying on a normal life. If the changes in our world are not those that lead to greater love, greater warmth with others, more caring, closer relationships, and a sense of central solidity within our own self, then we have been wasting our time.

The important thing about everyday life is that we get down and get on with it. We must strip away all this spiritual and mystical garbage. We must look at what is happening at the moment and deal with it. It is better that we forget all deliberations on the true, the good, the beautiful and our own development. Since we have been practising different meditation techniques in the background of our awareness, then the benefits of those practices stay with us and operate behind the scenes. We can only end up interfering with them by keeping them in mind during our normal everyday life. The task ever before us is to deal with whatever is present in the moment.

Each individual slice of reality around us contains its own fullness and richness of experience and challenge. If we do not meddle with our perception of that moment, we can react quite naturally to it with our full nature. In this way we ensure that we do what is required without distortion. This is not always an easy thing to do. We are distracted by thoughts, by musing, by ponderings. We mull over what is past. We rehearse what is to come. We get frustrated when things do not go our way. We become irritated when we are interrupted. We worry about events to come, feeling perhaps unprepared for the demands that we believe may be placed upon us.

Yet we are at all times our own selves in our totality. At every place and at every moment the whole universe is fully embodied right there and then. This is equally true of you yourself. Wherever you are during each and every moment, you embody your total being: you are totally present in each moment of your life. We are each fully present every place and every moment of our experience in the same way that the cosmos manifests totally in every place and at every moment of time. The mystics of old said that the microcosm was patterned in the same way as the macrocosm. We, of course, are not happy with this but take it upon ourselves to use our limited faculties to alter what must be and the course events might take, oblivious of the fact that we do not have enough information to properly make any such decisions. We are not always aware of all the factors in any given case, and we have nowhere near enough capacity for compassion and caring to decide upon events which influence the lives of others. We frequently have too little personal energy to put into effect our grand schemes, operating, as they often do, against the natural progression of the evolving cosmos.

There are many techniques which when diligently practised give us some control over events in the outside world. Some practitioners of these techniques have used their skills to ensure that traffic lights were set to green in the direction in which they were driving. This was almost invariably done without thought of consequence to the cross-traffic which, for all the knowledge such traffic-light magicians had, may well have included a doctor on an emergency call. Behind all developments and manifestations is an elementary harmony with which we may interfere, by deliberate use of our skills for our own purposes. Bear in mind that these may not only be selfish purposes, for the need to be of service to others can lead to just as much meddling in the natural unfolding of creation as the desire for a new washing machine. In the quietness of our own time, we use meditation techniques to work upon ourselves, but for the rest of our time we must place complete faith in the operation of our own nature in harmony with cosmic law. Whatever situation arises, we are there in our totality. The instinctive reaction in us is always the right one, provided that we allow it to flow into expression and give it those forms of expression which are suitable to its nature. In this way we will grow as a tree grows. We will build as coral builds. We shall remove the outworn like a landslide does. We shall wear down obstacles like a glacier. We shall run into union with the source of all, with the deliberate purpose of a river running into the sea.

The Exercise

The particular type of meditation for this final session is often accounted to be the most direct form that has been devised and to be the simplest to take up. Yet it is one of the most difficult to achieve. Its difficulty stems solely from its simplicity, for simplicity does not often appeal to the sophisticated mind of today's world. However, nothing ventured, nothing gained, so here is a description of the exercise for you to follow during the next practice session.

There are two tasks, each of which actually amounts to the same thing. The first half of the description is as follows:

— Whatever you are doing pay close unwavering attention to it.

The second half of the instruction, which balances this, runs:

— When thought prompts you to act, then act.

These two instructions operate in the following way. To begin with, this meditation is ideally carried out in your normal everyday life. It has no opening or closing gesture. It has no time set apart for its practice, for it is continual and ongoing. If you wish, however, you may set aside a certain period of the day when you will attempt to behave according to these instructions, relinquishing that practice for the remainder of the day. If you choose to do this then you should continue to use the beginning and ending gestures to mark off your practice from the time when you are not performing it.

Let us suppose that you are washing the dishes. To make this a meditation, you must wash the dishes with your whole being. Your thought should be on the dishes you are washing. Your perception, vision, feeling and hearing should all be directed towards the dishwashing – that process alone. Now let us suppose that there is a knock on the door. This is something which has arisen and to which you will attend. This you will do by choosing whether or not to answer the door. If you decide to open it then you will have finished with the dishwashing, even though that act may be incomplete. Now your whole attention and thought and being will be concentrated on communication with the people who have come to your door.

Let us suppose that instead of a knock at the door, you suddenly remembered that you had to plant some seeds in the garden. Immediately you would pay your whole attention to that thought and deal with it. If your memory is not what it should be, and this is true for many of us, then perhaps you would deal with it by leaving the dishwashing and writing a note to yourself to remind you of the seeds. However, a far more effective method of dealing with this type of interruption is to stop your dishwashing immediately and go out and plant the seeds. If, part-way through planting the seeds, you begin to worry about the dishes which have not been finished, then walk straight back inside and wash the dishes. The purpose of the meditation is simple. Whatever you are doing, be fully there with it. If you start to go somewhere else you must either bring your mind and attention back or follow and do it. The method is simplicity itself. The answer to every question that starts, 'What if...?' is always the same: Deal with it. Whatever you do, be fully there doing it. Keep at one with your actions in the world and your own being. Record your results in Table 9 as usual.

Table 9
Reality and concentration

General results

Special experiences

Most common difficulties

Summary

— The test of a realization is the change that occurs in the outside world.

— The universe is fully embodied at every point and every time.

— We too are always fully present in each moment of our experience, whether we are aware of it or not.

— We have the same pattern as the universe and cosmic law runs through our whole being when we do not 'meddle'.

— When fully trained we act correctly out of our true nature like a river running to the sea.

— Practise the exercise and record your results *before* proceeding further.

10
The Beginning

Feedback

What sort of experiences have you had over the last practice session? If you are anything like most people who have practised this system without previous experience, you will have had an interesting time. People's reactions to this meditation technique vary considerably, according to their own life situation and circumstances. However, there are probably two very common experiences that lie behind all others, both of which, in their own way, indicate that the method is having its effect. These experiences are as follows:

— At first I found that I was jumping about all over the place, but gradually I seemed to spend more time on each thing and seemed to have more time as well.
— I found I became so fully engrossed in what I was doing that I would suddenly realize I had lost all sense of self – that sounds had become sharper and sweeter and the whole world was full of light. As soon as I realized that it stopped.

Perhaps you had experiences similar to these. But if not, it may be that this method is not for you. Or perhaps you might like to consider trying it for a longer period.

The Beginning

You have now had experience of eight pure types of meditation which can be combined in numerous ways to produce a meditation practice suitable for almost any type of person. Indeed the practices of the various schools of mysticism and spiritual development generally operate in their early stages by giving their students a meditation method based upon a combination of two or three of the methods given here in this manual. By your own experience with these methods you will have come to a realization as to which of the practices are most suitable for your own development. These will be the exercises which seem to give you some positive result together with those that offer something of a challenge. You should form your choice of methods by combining those at which you were skilled with those at which you performed very poorly. These are the important poles – it is practically useless to take only those methods which made you 'feel good' or feel merely 'comfortable'. Please do not do this as you will be wasting a useful opportunity to pursue self-knowledge. Select carefully and build your own set of practices into your own personal system.

Where do you go from here? It is said in the mystical traditions that when the student is ready the teacher will appear. Remember that your teacher is always the teaching principle which responds to the teaching with which you come into contact. These teachings may come to you in many different forms. The teacher is not always a person. A book or a diagram, a picture, any form of symbolic representation of inner realities can be your teacher. The teachings you need will come to you in your life at a time when you are ready to appreciate them fully. Even where the teacher is a person, there often comes a time when the student has learned all there is to be learned from that person. Then it is time for such a student to pass on to another teacher able to take them further along the way, by providing them with that which they need. In such cases there is a gap of time between one teacher and the next. This is a very necessary period for the student to continue practising that which they have already learned.

If the teacher appears when you are ready, then your work is to make yourself always ready, to be prepared for that time. The exercises given here that you have experienced over the last few months may be combined and practised as a personal meditation technique. If you are sincere and practise regularly and frequently, you will be preparing yourself for those who can teach you further. Steadfast practice of your personal meditation method will lead you in ways along which stand those who may guide you further on your quest of self-realization. The exercises in this handbook are given in the hope that they have at least helped to start you on your journey. In that journey may you enjoy every success, and the attainment of your own personal grail.

Table 10
Changes experienced since beginning to practise meditation

Inner (my self, my values, my reactions, etc.)

Outer (my environment, circumstances, etc.)

These have resulted in:

I obtained from my practices:

The Exercise

The exercise for the next period has three parts.

Part One
Write down in Table 10 as carefully as you can what changes have occurred since you began practising these exercises and what you have obtained from them.

Part Two
Look back at the results of your first exercise where you recorded your hopes and goals. Compare your aims with the changes that have occurred. Now apply the tests you devised for success or failure.

How did you fare? Many people find that they gain valuable results from meditation exercises which they could neither predict nor appreciate before taking up their practice. If often happens that what was desired at first is obtained as a little-valued side-effect after regular and sustained practice. Sometimes, in the light of experience with these exercises, some goals become no longer relevant and the need for these falls away quite naturally.

There are many variations, but one thing that the majority of practitioners of this course agree upon is that the use of these exercises brings a firsthand appreciation of what meditation 'is'. This is the whole point of the course, for even though all the experiences in the world cannot lead to understanding without knowledge, knowledge itself can never be a substitute for experience.

Part Three
Now it is your turn to take over for a while and build your own meditation method. Start by compiling a list of your practices, noting those which brought strong results, those which seemed difficult, those which were merely 'nice', and so on. Take the most effective and the most challenging styles and combine them into one or two separate practices. Wherever possible when joining your meditations together, keep them in the order in which they were presented to you.

In addition, it is often useful to begin each session with at least some relaxation and rhythmic breathing, even if these are not among your choices. A sample daily exercise may then work out like one of the following:

Example One
Opening gesture
Relaxation
Breathing, counting
Middle pillar exercise
Guided fantasy
Closing gesture

Example Two
Opening gesture
Relaxation
Breathing
Mantra
Silent devotion
Closing gesture
(Evening) Offering of music

Example Three

(Morning)	Opening gesture
	Direct attention for 30 minutes
	Closing gesture
(Evening)	Opening gesture
	Chinese energy meditation
	T'ai Chi Ch'uan mudra
	Closing gesture

Your ingenuity will be able to devise a programme for your own development and needs from these few illustrations of the method. May your quest be ever fruitful.

Appendix A
Group Work

It is possible to use this manual as the basis for the group study and practice of meditation. Meetings may be held once each fortnight, or month, where experiences are shared and the material within a given chapter discussed. The exercise is then practised by all in the intervening time before the next meeting.

The Organizer

We first begin by asking what sort of person can run a workshop of this type. It should go without saying that results obtained will depend upon the familiarity of the organizer with the meditation techniques presented. This does not mean, however, that the organizer must be a long-time meditator. There is no reason why a group of beginners could not work from the material in this book provided they were able to arrange for the duties of organizer to be performed amongst themselves.

The whole idea of such a workshop approach is to give each participant an opportunity to share his or her experiences with the other members of the group. Valuable insights into the meditation processes can be obtained in this way even without an expert, provided several points are observed.

— Every experience is valid.
— No 'interpretation', criticism or 'judging' should be permitted.
— The agreed meeting format should be adhered to.
— Everyone has the right to keep experiences private.
— Records should be kept – both group and individual.
— No one has a right answer for any but themselves.

To ensure that these conditions are met there should be a specific workshop leader able to remind the members of these conditions when it seems they are being violated. The leader of course may be a different person at each session.

On the other hand, where there is an organizer available who has had considerable meditation experience – say, more than five years, then that person should be able to bring additional insights to expand and enhance the experiences of the other group members. Here the leader must be careful not to impute their own values and interpretations upon the other members whilst at the same time contributing their own extensive experience to that of the group.

Course Structure

There are two aspects to the structure of a workshop: the administrative organization of the people attending and the selection and organization of the material that is to be presented. I have already dealt to some extent with the first aspect in discussing the workshop organizer and the qualities required there – the keynotes are participation and acceptance.

We come then to the structure of the individual sessions. To a large extent the specific programme should be agreed upon by all the participants at the first session. It should also be open for the structure of each session to be reviewed and changed if found wanting. One agenda that has been found particularly useful and one which you might like to adapt for your own purposes is given below. It could provide a starting point or a foundation upon which to build a structure that matches the needs of those participating in *your* workshop.

Sample Agenda

Social time
Before you start off in earnest, reserve a few minutes for social chit-chat. This helps the participants relax in the new setting at which they have just arrived.

Declared start
It is important to arrange some method to signal that the session will 'formally' begin. It need not be as heavy-handed as striking a large gong with a great crash. What is necessary is to show clearly to those present that the work for the evening is now going to start.

Feedback
The first item is for each person in turn – if they wish – to share with the group the experiences they encountered in using the method of meditation decided

upon for the preceding period. This should be encouraged and warmly and openly received. Honesty should be fostered by ensuring that no responses are ever ridiculed or discounted. Every experience is valid. It is a response of that person at that time to that exercise and is valuable data if the group is to seriously understand what the meditational processes are all about.

Warm-ups
The degree of talking that goes on during feedback will usually result in a drop in the energy levels of the participants. This is partly because each person has 'held the floor' in turn and reported to a relatively captive audience. So here we raise the energy levels again with one or two 'games'. These can be chosen from the awareness and sensitivity material that is on the market and known to the group participants. Another source of games is the 'Life be in it' material – the game called 'Knots' is a particularly good one. The essentials are movement, full involvement and physical contact. Plus the use of the imagination!

Cross-chatter
Now that everyone is feeling enthused, a discussion can be started to comment and evaluate upon the experiences that have been reported. Here it is the group's task to make consistent sense of the data shared rather than to evaluate each other's performance on the exercises. Naturally there can be tensions and conflicts in these situations. The essential point is to ensure that criticism is not directed at individuals but rather directed to the discrepancies and anomalies noted. It is the work of the group as a whole to resolve these. Sometimes this may mean that the discussion is postponed until the members can do some 'reading up' on the subject in some area. Keep the group goals in mind throughout.

Feed-forward
Now the type of meditation to be practised over the next period is described or presented by the person who is responsible for the job on this particular evening. A brief outline is given of what the meditation is and what it is not, together with a few suggestions as to where it is used.

Practice
The meditation for the next period is now tried out by all the participants together. This is necessary to check that everyone has understood the process and that any potential difficulties have been resolved beforehand.

Warm-ups (optional)
If energy is low again, try another game.

Administration
Time and place of next meeting must be specified if not clearly understood by all present.

Refreshment
Tea, coffee, herbal teas, biscuits, cake, etc. as desired. More social chat.

This agenda can be left fairly flexible. There have been times when it has taken one and a half hours to get through it and other times when it has taken three hours. It all depends on the group, the method, the evening, and so on.

A record should be kept of each session. It is a good idea to prepare for each participant at the end of the workshop series a set of papers showing the results obtained for each meditation type. They may then keep this with their own records for comparison purposes.

Another point about records is that each participant should be encouraged to keep their own record of practices. If this is not done, it is virtually impossible to give an accurate report of experiences during the 'feedback' session. The individual experiences would tend to be coloured by the reports that other people had previously given.

For the first session there will not, of course, be any feedback. It is essential that the tone of the whole workshop series be set at this first meeting, so instead of the feedback session you should arrange a special period in which the participants can get to know each other. It is also a good idea at this time to establish with each person what it is they hope to get out of the workshop. The following suggestion is one way you as organizer might run this particular session.

A Sample Session

Have each person give their name to the group and to say how they came to hear of the workshop. This can be arranged with the 'conch shell' approach if many of the participants are strangers to each other – you provide some object of a size to fit in the palm of the hand and such that it can be easily and safely tossed from one person to another. A small bean-bag would do very well, as would a light piece of wood of smooth shape, or a rag-doll, perhaps (use ingenuity here). Now you explain that the person in possession of the object has the floor. When they have finished introducing themself they should toss the object to another person at random and preferably someone they do not already know; you could suggest that it would be someone they would *like* to know or someone perhaps that they know but would like to know better. In this way each person has a chance to introduce themself without knowing precisely when they are going to be called on to speak to the group. They also have something in the hand to hold and feel in case they are somewhat anxious.

Don't introduce yourself in this way but wait for the object to come to you as the others do. It is interesting to see whether you are left until last or not.

Now, once this has happened and people have loosened up a bit, follow up with the next exercise. Divide the workshop into pairs. You can participate or not as required to make up an even number. One member of each pair tells their partner, say, two things they want to get out of the workshop. The listener must not make notes but must be sure they have heard exactly what their partner has said by repeating it back if necessary. The roles are then reversed. Set a time limit for this. Give each one the same amount of time. At the end each person in turn states their partner's needs to the whole group. You should record these on a large sheet or board in such a way that all can see them. Progress through until you have recorded everyone's requirements. Invite the group to note similarities and differences, thereby arriving at groupings. This exercise in fact starts the series of practices itself. The workshop participants may then work upon their success and failure tests for the second meeting.

The session leader must try to keep a close watch upon the needs of the participants. People generally find it difficult both to participate and monitor. If insufficient monitoring is going on, so that some people are not being heard or valued properly, this task should be carried out by the leader. Of course, there is nothing to prevent the leader afterwards pointing out the lack of attention. It should not fall upon the same person to monitor each time there is a meeting.

Participating in such a workshop can be a rewarding and enlightening experience but it requires skills and a delicacy that challenges the resources.

Appendix B
Further Pathworkings

An excellent introduction to the method of *unstructured* pathworkings is given by Edwin Steinbecher in *The Inner Guide Meditation* (Aquarian Press, England). The practices given in that book are the basis for a lifetime of study. This approach can be supplemented by following the suggestions given by J.H. Brennan in *Astral Doorways* (Weiser).

Structured pathworkings are, however, a little more difficult to come by. Many books on the 'popular psychologies' contain fantasy journeys and these are of varying value, to the extent that they include or fail to include archetypal themes. Many pathworkings are provided by the Western mystical schools for the exclusive and restricted use of their members and students. Fortunately, however, this situation is changing and more may be published now than previously. Three books that provide excellent examples are Marian Green's *Paths of Magic* (Quest, England) and Dolores Ashcroft-Nowicki's *Highways of the Mind* (Servants of the Light, Jersey, Channel Islands) and *The Shining Paths* (Aquarian Press, England). These should lead you on to other sources. The present author is also preparing a set of pathworkings for publication.

A rich storehouse of pathworking material is embodied in the myths and legends of many times and cultures. When you have been practising these techniques for one or two years, then you will be suitably qualified to write your own from these resources. This should not occur thoughtlessly, though, for you should not create for yourself or others a pathworking that you do not understand.

Bibliography

It would be impossible to list all the books that have in their way helped me to the realizations that are set out here. In any case, this would only be a list of the things that had triggered patterns within me. You are a unique individual and as such you will have your own set of triggers for those realizations which lead to your greater growth and unfolding. Books are a kind of food, and like different plants, or the same plant types in different locations, we each need our own special 'diet' to bring out the fullest unfolding of which we are capable.

Bibliographies serve two purposes at least. It is very common for someone who is about to read a book to check the bibliography first. If they see there enough of the books they have already read and, what is more, with which they have agreed or to which they have felt attuned, then the book might be accepted as useful. In this way, there will be little challenge to the set of ideas and practices that they have made their own. In many cases this is useful - for those who already have a regular set of practices, or who are committed to a given world view through the tradition of their training. In many more cases, though, it provides a guarantee of safety and comfort. The first type of people will know this book by its contents. The second type will find that that guarantee is not forthcoming.

Another use of bibliographies is to provide pointers to those places where themes may be more fully developed. This is very helpful, for through these the meditator may extend their practice and gain the knowledge that will form the basis of further understanding.

You will find, however, that if you pursue the practices given here, with dedication and care, those things you need for your unfolding will come into your life automatically. This applies not only to events but also to books, workshops, talks, radio shows, music, individuals and so forth.

Lists of books are in this regard superfluous. If any book would help, then you have already read it, or will do after practising your exercises. If it would mislead, then you will encounter that for yourself without it being offered here.

However, although these things will come into your life by a law of attraction, you must still recognize the opportunity for yourself. You must know when to act on the inner promptings of the spirit within. Your practices will bring you to this knowledge and to the ability to convert that knowledge into action.

It is in the sincere belief, based upon experience, that you will find this so for yourself that this book is offered.

Index